Europe and Islam

This book provides an in-depth analysis of the challenging relationship between Europe and Islam. The general chapters on secularism, security, identity and solidarity show the challenge of promoting a stable multicultural society. In-depth analysis of France, Germany, Britain, the Netherlands and Italy reveals the extent to which this challenge of stable multiculturalism differs from one country to the next. The argument that emerges is not that Europe and Islam are incompatible. Rather, it is that reconciling the tensions that arise from the mixing of different cultures will require enormous patience, understanding and investment. The contributors represent some of the leading voices in debates about European politics, and not just those focusing narrowly on the question of Islam. Hence, this volume offers both a gateway to understanding the special relationship between Europe and the Muslim world and a means of tying that understanding to the future of European integration. This book was previously published as a special issue of *The International Spectator*.

Erik Jones is a Professor of European Studies and International Political Economy at the Johns Hopkins School of Advanced International Studies and a Senior Research Fellow at Nuffield College, Oxford.

Saskia van Genugten is the author of *Libya in Western Foreign Policies* (2016). She has a PhD degree in European Studies from SAIS Johns Hopkins University and currently works as a UAE-based researcher.

T0351661

Europe and Islam

Edited by
Erik Jones and Saskia van Genugten

Routledge
Taylor & Francis Group

LONDON AND NEW YORK

First published 2016 by Routledge

2 Park Square, Milton Park, Abingdon, Oxfordshire OX14 4RN
711 Third Avenue, New York, NY 10017

Routledge is an imprint of the Taylor & Francis Group, an informa business

First issued in paperback 2018

British Library Cataloguing in Publication Data
A catalogue record for this book is available from the British Library

ISBN 13: 978-1-138-67112-6 (hbk)
ISBN 13: 978-1-138-39253-3 (pbk)

Typeset in Adobe Garamond Pro
by diacriTech, Chennai

Publisher's Note
The publisher accepts responsibility for any inconsistencies that may have arisen during the conversion of this book from journal articles to book chapters, namely the possible inclusion of journal terminology.

Disclaimer
Every effort has been made to contact copyright holders for their permission to reprint material in this book. The publishers would be grateful to hear from any copyright holder who is not here acknowledged and will undertake to rectify any errors or omissions in future editions of this book.

Contents

CONTENTS

Citation Information

The chapters in this book were originally published in *The International Spectator*, volume 48, issue 1 (March 2013). When citing this material, please use the original page numbering for each article, as follows:

Introduction
Erik Jones and Saskia van Genugten
The International Spectator, volume 48, issue 1 (March 2013) pp. 1–4

Chapter 1
Secularism and Islam: The Theological Predicament
Olivier Roy
The International Spectator, volume 48, issue 1 (March 2013) pp. 5–19

Chapter 2
EU Foreign Policy and Political Islam: Towards a New Entente in the Post-Arab Spring Era?
Timo Behr
The International Spectator, volume 48, issue 1 (March 2013) pp. 20–33

Chapter 3
The French Debate on National Identity and the Sarkozy Presidency: A Retrospective
Jonathan Laurence and Gabriel Goodliffe
The International Spectator, volume 48, issue 1 (March 2013), pp. 34–47

Chapter 4
Muslim Organisations and Intergenerational Change in Germany
Dirk Halm
The International Spectator, volume 48, issue 1 (March 2013) pp. 48–57

CITATION INFORMATION

Chapter 5
Muslims in Italy: The Need for an 'Intesa' with the Italian State
Karim Mezran
The International Spectator, volume 48, issue 1 (March 2013) pp. 58–71

Chapter 6
The Netherlands and Islam: In Defence of Liberalism and Progress?
Saskia van Genugten
The International Spectator, volume 48, issue 1 (March 2013) pp. 72–85

Chapter 7
Islam and Muslim Communities in the UK: Multiculturalism, Faith and Security
Catherine Fieschi and Nick Johnson
The International Spectator, volume 48, issue 1 (March 2013) pp. 86–101

Chapter 8
Identity, Solidarity, and Islam in Europe
Erik Jones
The International Spectator, volume 48, issue 1 (March 2013) pp. 102–116

For any permission-related enquiries please visit:
http://www.tandfonline.com/page/help/permissions

Notes on Contributors

Timo Behr currently works as a consultant based in the Middle East.

Catherine Fieschi is the Director of Counterpoint, London, UK.

Saskia van Genugten currently works as a UAE-based researcher.

Gabriel Goodliffe is a Professor of International Relations and International Political Economy at the Instituto Tecnológico Autónomo de México, Mexico.

Dirk Halm is an Associate Professor at the Centre for Studies on Turkey and Integration Research at Duisburg-Essen University, and teaches Political Sociology at Münster University, Germany.

Nick Johnson is the Chief Executive of the British Educational Research Association and a Fellow of the Smith Institute in London.

Erik Jones is a Professor of European Studies and International Political Economy at the Johns Hopkins School of Advanced International Studies and a Senior Research Fellow at Nuffield College, Oxford.

Jonathan Laurence is a Professor of Political Science at Boston College and Non-resident Senior Fellow at the Brookings Institution.

Karim Mezran is a Senior Fellow at the Rafik Hariri Center for the Middle East at the Atlantic Council of the United States.

Olivier Roy is a Professor of Social and Political Theory and the Head of the Mediterranean Programme at the Robert Schuman Centre for Advanced Studies, European University Institute, San Domenico di Fiesole, Italy.

Introduction

Erik Jones and Saskia van Genugten

Postwar Europe is committed to equality, non-discrimination and individual dignity. Nevertheless, recent trends across Europe suggest that commitment is starting to erode. The integration of a large number of immigrants from Islamic countries has been challenging. Sometimes, the political response has been excessive. The Council of Europe, Amnesty International and Human Rights Watch have called upon European governments to oppose bills aimed at restricting Islamic customs, such as the use of the full veil, ritual slaughtering and the building of minarets.[1] In the words of the Council of Europe's Human Rights Commissioner, Thomas Hammarberg, what is needed is nothing less than a "European Spring to overcome old and emerging forms of racism and intolerance".[2]

This is hardly the first time that Europe has experienced challenges in its relationship with Islam. However, the recent change in the pattern and volume of immigration into Europe from Islamic countries makes a qualitative difference. For centuries, Islamic communities dwelled in the European periphery, but only in the past decades have several strains of Islam introduced themselves in the continent's core, its main cities and its political hearts. In a very short period of time, Islam has become a European religion. In fact, Islam is Europe's fastest growing religion and also the second largest after Christianity. The exact number of 'Muslims' in Europe is difficult to estimate, due to imperfect registration methods. Nevertheless, the trend lines are clear. According to one of the more reliable counts, Europe had 29.6 million Muslims in 1990 (4.1 percent of its total population), which grew to 44.1 million in 2010 (6.0 percent of its total population) and

---

[1] See, for example, Amnesty Report, *Choice and Prejudice: Discrimination against Muslims in Europe*, 2012, http://www.amnesty.nl/sites/default/files/public/religious_discrm_muslims_report.pdf, and Human Rights Watch, *World Report 2012: European Union*, January 2012, http://www.hrw.org/sites/default/files/related_material/eu_2012.pdf.

[2] Council of Europe, "Anti-Muslim Prejudice Hinders Integration", Press release CommDH034(2012), 24 July 2012, https://wcd.coe.int/ViewDoc.jsp?Ref=CommDH-PR034(2012)&Language=lanEnglish&Ver=original&Site=DC&BackColorInternet=F5CA75&BackColorIntranet=F5CA75&BackColorLogged=A9BACE.

is predicted to reach 58.2 million by 2030 (8.0 percent of its total population).[3] Moreover, the demographic structure of this immigration enhances its impact: by 2030, around 42 percent of Europe's Muslims will be under 30 years old. For the non-Muslim population, this is expected to be only 31 percent.

It is no surprise therefore that one of today's main social questions is how Europeans should respond to the influx of this new, organised life-philosophy into everyday life. The answer is neither self-evident nor innocuous. Not everyone views immigration as positive, as is clear from the rise of anti-immigration parties. For some, scepticism about a more diverse society is based on an idea (not necessarily a truth) that life was better before the age of mass immigration. Others are wary about seeing immigrant populations strain their already limited welfare-state resources, arguing that it is unfair for newcomers to have equal entitlement to state services and benefits even though they did not contribute to building them up. Still others justify attacks on Islamic practices as a legitimate defence against 'intolerance', arguing that anti-immigrant policies are necessary to preserve progressive values such as secularism or individual freedoms, including those of women, homosexuals and even animals. No doubt, a fringe group of Europeans simply dislikes other cultures, full stop.

The purpose of this special issue is to explore the many aspects of the relationship between Europe and Islam. The goal is to provide insights to help policymakers navigate the current debate – to recognise where there are simple misunderstandings and where there are real problems to be solved. For example, many European policymakers treat the Islam in Europe debate as part of a larger quest for identity in a globalising and individualising world, as a manifestation of cultural defence. This seems to hold true for both Islamic constituencies as well as non-Islamic constituencies in Europe. However, by doing so these same policymakers end up formatting Islam as a European religion. In turn, this leads to misunderstandings about who speaks for Islam, how Islamic communities are organised, and where the best points of contact for creating dialogue lie. This argument emerges in the paper by Olivier Roy.

Another tendency is to recast Islam and immigrants from the Islamic world as some sort of security problem. Almost everywhere in Europe, policymakers have begun not only to promote stricter rules for immigration and integration, but also to focus on Islamic practices as a source of social problems. How then should European foreign policymakers react to the call for freedom, democracy and dignity so clearly discerned in the early stages of the Arab uprisings that started at the end of 2010? And how should they react to the democratically chosen new Islamoriented leaders? This challenge is addressed by Timo Behr.

---

[3] The Pew Forum, "The Future of the Global Muslim Population", January 2011, http://www.pewforum. org/future-of-the-global-muslim-population-regional-europe.aspx#ftn34.

The security dimension of the Europe and Islam debate is important. Events in the Arabic world influence the way Europeans consider the democratic and liberal credentials of their own national Muslim co-nationals. Nevertheless, while the big questions of identity, solidarity and fundamental values tend to surface in all countries, country-specificities abound. After all, individual European states have approached Islam in ways that reflect specific intra-European variations in church-state relations, state-minority relations, colonial histories, national identities, as well as differences in social welfare systems, electoral systems and geographic location. In addition, the state of the art of research and analysis on the domestic situation differs from country to country. The authors of the country cases in this collection had the liberty to pick the approach considered most appropriate for their specific country, in order to reflect best the idiosyncratic debate. Hence Jonathan Laurence and Gabriel Goodliffe focus on the identity debate provoked by Nicolas Sarkozy in France, Dirk Halm examines the discourse surrounding second and third generation immigrants in Germany, Karim Mezran looks at attempts to negotiate an *intesa* between the state and the Islamic communities in Italy, Saskia van Genugten examines the rise of anti-immigrant populism in the Netherlands, and Catherine Fieschi and Nick Johnson look at the reaction to immigrant sponsored terrorism in the United Kingdom.

An overarching element seems to be that in the past decade, the national models of immigration and integration that used to bring communities together have begun to reveal weaknesses. The multicultural model such as was known in the UK and the Netherlands has been scorned for creating parallel societies, providing a *carte blanche* for more extremist strains of religious thought and dangerously eroding social cohesion. In reaction, minorities are increasingly asked to be more like the majority and are expected to prove this for example through language command requirements and culture tests showing a basic 'ability' to embrace the dominant set of values. France, on the other hand, witnesses the limitations of the ideal of assimilating minority cultures to a strictly defined national identity.

In all such cases, the conflicts are about rules and accepted practices in the shared public space. Islam has brought a new set of values to the arena, thereby testing the limits and definition of concepts such as liberalism, tolerance and freedom of speech, whose validity until recently had been taken for granted in postwar Europe. At the same time, Muslims in Europe struggle to define the ways in which they can best practice their religion in a non-Islamic space. The lingering question is about the extent to which differing 'fundamental' principles and values can exist next to each other. This is the question addressed by Erik Jones.

The conclusion to the debate is not written. European politics has a long way to go before it adapts fully to the presence of Islamic immigrants; Europeans will work long to stabilise relations with Islamic countries on their borders as well. There is nothing surprising in the predicament. But successful reconciliation cannot be taken for granted either. It is necessary to take stock of the situation, measure progress and regress, and look for new ways to move forward.

This special issue is one such stock-taking effort. It would not have been possible without the very generous support of the Wendy's-Arby's Group Foundation and the Jack and Carol Wasserman Fund. The original drafts of these papers were presented as part of a research seminar at The Johns Hopkins University SAIS in Bologna. The authors benefited from several rounds of comments from a talented group of students, including Geoffrey Cailloux, Hayat Essakkati, Mitko Grigorov, Allison Hart and Sarah Hexter. They also drew support from presentations made by, *inter alia*, Tariq Ramadan, Susanna Mancini and Meltem Müftüler-Bac. The participation of these scholars in the wider conversation generated by the project is gratefully acknowledged. Finally, thanks go to Gabriele Tonne and her colleagues at the Istituto Affari Internazionali (IAI) for their patient and constructive commentary. Such projects are necessarily collaborative and while the mistakes usually come from the authors, the insights often come from those who seek no credit for their involvement. This special issue is no different.

Secularism and Islam: The Theological Predicament

Olivier Roy

Does the integration of Islam in Europe presuppose a prior 'religious reformation' that would make Islam compatible with so-called 'European values'? The wave of religious revival that has touched the new generations of Muslims in Europe is not a return to traditional religious practices but, on the contrary, a recasting of religious norms and values in a European context. Fundamentalism means deculturation. What we are witnessing is a complex, and often tense, process of formatting Islam into a Western model of relationship between state, religion and society. But this process is taking place precisely at a time when Europe is not sure about its own identity: what does a 'European Christian identity' mean when churches are increasingly empty? Faith and culture have never been so disconnected.

Does the integration of Islam in Europe presuppose a prior 'religious reformation' that would make Islam compatible with so-called 'European values'? And what are these European values? Are they Christian values or secular values? While all European constitutions and treaties stress the commitment towards 'human rights', 'religious freedom' and 'democracy', the status of 'secularism' is more complex. If we define secularism as the separation of state and religion, this is not the case in many European countries which grant a specific status to one or more recognised religions (for example, England, Italy and Germany). If secularism is taken to mean that the religious reference is more and more irrelevant in society, daily life and culture, accompanied by a decrease in individual religious practices, which is the case in all European countries, then Europe is certainly secular. But in this case, secular values conflict with Christian ones: issues like abortion, contraception and gay marriages are largely opposing 'believers' on one hand, and 'non-believers' on the other. How can we refer to the Christian roots of secular Europe if Europe's values contradict the teachings of the Church?

Going beyond the debate on Christian identity, however, there is a large consensus that the huge Muslim population that has recently settled in Europe creates a specific challenge, because Islam may not be compatible with either the Christian identity of Europe or its secularism. The debate is framed indifferently in cultural terms (Western culture versus Oriental culture) or religious terms (Christian Europe versus Islam) as Islam is seen as an all-encompassing religion in which there is no distinction between politics, religion and culture. But such an approach, by essentializing Islam as a closed and atemporal system of thought, ignores the concrete practices of real Muslims and their interaction with a European society which is itself complex and often divided on many central issues.

This article intends to address the premises that more or less openly underlie the public policies of European governments and local authorities when dealing with the issue of 'integrating' Islam, either by making room for (authorising the building of mosques), or conversely, restraining Muslim religious practices (occasionally banning burqas and veils). Both attitudes, although in opposition, contribute to 'formatting' the religious practices of Muslims, which means adapting them to an environment in which culture does not play a mediating role between the individual believer and society. Traditional cultures are fading away among the new generations of immigrants who, by the way, are no longer migrants; nevertheless, they are in many instances experiencing a religious revival which entails a recasting of religious markers and norms disconnected from the pristine cultures. So the issue is clearly about 'religion' and less and less about culture. This is why multiculturalism is increasingly irrelevant, and why the issue is ever more associated with a debate on what makes up the theological core of Islam as a religion. This is what is referred to here as the 'theological predicament'.

The vain essentialisation of Islam

An ongoing debate about Islam in Europe deals with the 'compatibility' of Islam with so-called European values: is Islam compatible with (take your pick)... democracy, secularism, human rights (more exactly women's rights, gay rights, etc.). This is the theological predicament: the issue of integrating Muslims in Europe is supposed to be linked to an enquiry into the theological tenets of Islam as a religion. Either the Muslims present and promote a liberal interpretation of Islam, or their integration in Europe is conditioned on a prior theological reform that would make Islam compatible with (once more) so-called Western values. Such a view is also promoted by 'liberal' Muslims, like Irshad Manji, a Canadian journalist and essayist, while former Muslims turned atheist like Ayaan Hirsi Ali or

Ibn Warraq are more pessimistic: they have doubts about the possibility of reforming Islam. The media regularly highlight the plight of some 'moderate' Muslim thinker who has to be promoted and encouraged in opposition to his fellow believers: in France, for instance, local imams like Soheib Ben Cheykh[1] in Marseille or Hassen Chalghoumi[2] in Seine-Saint-Denis are featured as lonely reformists coming under attack from fundamentalist groups. Irshad Manji has even been compared to Martin Luther.[3] Some Muslim thinkers or leaders declare themselves to be the long awaited Muslim reformer that the West desperately needs: in a speech given in Great Britain, Tahir ul Qadri, leader of a Pakistani religious movement, presented himself as the first Muslim leader to have written the definitive fatwa against terrorism.[4]

This essentialist perception lies in the background of not only many stories reported by journalists (from polygamy and honour killings to terrorism) but also policies implemented by governments and administrations. Endless debates on "what does the Qur'an say?", not to speak about "what does the Qur'an *really* say?" fill blogs and conferences.[5] The debate about the burqa hinges on the same question: is the burqa nothing more than the fullest expression of a basic tenet of Islam (the seclusion of women) or is the burqa alien to the true spirit of Islam. In the end, all this means is that the burqa can be banned either because it is seen as an excessive but true expression of Islam, or because it is not an expression of Islam at all. But in both cases, the debate is about Islam, not about the personal and private decision of a given woman to wear the burqa.

However, this essentialist approach presents many legal and methodological hurdles that will be presented here. First of all, it challenges the separation of church and state and, paradoxically, the supposedly secular nature of the European state, because the state seems to consider interfering with religious creeds a duty. Second, it supposes that Europe's political culture is based on a set of premises shared among Europeans, including Christian believers. Third, it sees Islam as a timeless set of norms and values that are inscribed in the mind of every Muslim, even non-believers, who in this case are 'acted on' by an Islamic

---

[1] Author of *Marianne et le Prophète*, in which he defines a "republican Islam" compatible with the French *laïcité*.

[2] "Hassen Chalghoumi, un imam pas comme les autres", *Le Point.fr*, 26 January 2010. "An Imam unlike the others" because he is a moderate as the article points out. http://www.lepoint.fr/actualites-societe/2010-01-26/hassen-chalghoumi-un-imam-pas-comme-les-autres/920/0/417413.

[3] She wrote *The Trouble With Islam Today: A Muslim's Call for Reform in Her Faith*, and when awarded a PhD *honoris causa* by the University of Puget Sound in Tacoma, Washington, she was greeted with these words by Sunil Kukreja, Professor and Chair, Comparative Sociology, "Now the Director of the Moral Courage Project at New York University, your courage has drawn comparisons to Dietrich Bonhoeffer and Aleksandr Solzhenitsyn, to Martin Luther and Salman Rushdie, to Gloria Steinem and Betty Friedan."

[4] D. Casciani, "Islamic Scholar Tahir ul-Qadri Issues Terrorism Fatwa", *BBC News*, 2 March 2010. For a critical response to this fatwa, see T. Heneghan, "Tahir ul-Qadri and the Difficulty of Reporting on Fatwas", *Reuter FaithWorld*, 2 March 2010.

[5] Just Google the expression and look at the results.

'culture', culture here being little more than 'cold' religion. Therefore, the issue is to ensure the compatibility of these norms with so-called Western values or their national sub-sets. Yet, this approach ignores the daily practices of the various believers who do not care about writing a new treatise of Islamic theology, but simply adapt their own practices to a different environment, recast norms in terms of values, and try to find a common paradigm of 'faith' and religiosity with believers of other faiths, while leaving the theological framework of Islam almost intact. Incidentally, one should be careful about advocating reformation in religion. Many people who dream about seeing the coming of a Muslim Martin Luther have never read Martin Luther (and would be appalled by the '(in)compatibility' of his views with our Western values).

Reforming Islam through the state

Most public policies are driven by this 'theological predicament'. To give just one example, it is the underlying rational for stressing the need to train 'good' imams. Even countries where the separation of church and state is enshrined in the constitution are desperately trying to organise the training of imams: the French government subsidizes a course at the Catholic Institute of Paris, after having tried to set up an efficient representative body that could undertake the training (the body, *Conseil Français du Culte Musulman*, exists but is not effective). In the German Land of North Rhine-Westphalia, the local authorities have themselves established the curriculum of religious courses for Islam in public schools. The British government subsidizes the Quilliam Foundation (which aims at "developing a Muslim identity at home in, and with the West" and, more boldly, "reprogramming British Muslims").[6] Another alternative is to grant recognition to branches of Islam that appear more 'moderate' than mainstream Sunnism: for instance, Alevism among the Turks in Germany. Sufism is regularly presented as more open than most orthodox schools. The issue is particularly important at the local level where mayors are confronted with requests from Islamic associations to allow the building of mosques; before granting the authorisation they usually endeavour to vet the association or its leaders to see if they are moderate.

But this interventionism runs against the very concept of religious freedom. Whatever the legal system in Europe, it is usually admitted that a modern democratic secular state should ensure freedom of religion and not interfere with religious practices as long as they do not infringe on others' freedom or break the law.

Of course, this quest for moderate Muslims has regularly been justified after 9/11 by the fear of letting extremists take control of local mosques and have them recruit activists. But this legitimate fear of terrorism is also caught up in the

---

[6] See the report, *Re-Programming British Muslims*.

'theological predicament': the premise is that the more radical a believer is in his religious attitudes, the more radical he may become in his political activities. The issue is twofold: how can we define religious 'extremism'? And what is the relation between religious extremism and political radicalism?

The only legal argument for the state to curb certain religious practices would be the existence of a connection between 'religious practice' and violence: the more you pray, the more prone you are to perpetrating terrorist acts. In France, Muslim employees vetted for security clearance at Paris Charles De Gaulle airport are routinely asked about the frequency of their mosque attendance. This feeling is so internalised that a regular argument to deny that a neighbour or relative has terrorist links is to stress his/her lack of religious observance.[7]

The only reason for which a secular state can contemplate prohibiting the public display of a specific religious practice is for public order, without making any statement about what a religion is or should be. To define what is normal and what is extreme in terms of religious practices is beyond the scope of the modern democratic state. Nevertheless, it is deeply entrenched in the minds and practices of many politicians and is also advocated by public opinion: even in liberal Great Britain, the majority of the population would support a ban on wearing the burqa in public.

But to what extent does radical religious thinking lead to violence or terrorism? Are burqa wearing women more prone to go for jihad? No data support the idea for instance that wearing a burqa is a first step to political violence: there are, interestingly enough, more and more women (most of them converts) joining Al Qaeda (Muriel Degauque, Malika Arroud), but none of them have been known to wear the burqa. By the same token, the Salafi 'uniform' (long white *shalwar* and *qamis*, white skull cap, etc.) is not in use among Al Qaeda activists. In fact, most studies show that strict religious practice is not a hallmark of Al Qaeda activists.[8] This focus on the theological content of Islam and on religious observance is, in fact, a legacy of the European political culture and not of Islamic politics, culture or faith.

State and religion in Europe: a long history of violence and tensions

The debate on Islam does not come out of the blue: it is closely linked to the centuries-old debate on the role of religion in society and politics. If, confronted with Islam, the French stress the prevalence of secularism and the Italians the

---

[7] Abderazak Besseghir, a baggage handler at Roissy airport, was falsely accused in December 2002 of hiding weapons and explosives in his car, and the family objected that he does not practice his religion. For testimonies of other baggage handlers interrogated by the police on their religious practices, see "Nouvelles révélations dans l''affaire des bagagistes de Roissy", *SaphirNews*, 26 Oct 2006, http://www.saphirnews.com/Nouvelles-revelations-dans-l-affaire-des-bagagistes-de-Roissy_a4973.html.

[8] Sageman, *Understanding Terrorist Networks*.

leading role of Christianity, it is not because they have a different view of Islam, it is because they have a different view of religion. The search for a 'good Islam' does not embody a struggle between a liberal and secular Europe versus a foreign and fundamentalist religion (Islam). It re-enacts an age-old struggle inside Europe on the role of religion. What is at stake here is not so much Islam's compatibility with secularism as the definition, or more exactly the construction of secularism as a legal, cultural and political concept in the West.

If we look at history, neither secularism nor the separation of church and state is the product of European values based on the philosophy of the Enlightenment; rather, each is a political compromise, that may often have progressively turned into a consensus, to end religious wars. Such compromises have been established along national paradigms, which differ considerably from one European country to another. In fact, each European country has been able to achieve a stable compromise about the relationship between religion and politics after an initial period of violence and religious wars that lasted for centuries. Reformation in the early 16th century meant the breakdown of the religious unity of Europe. It entailed decades of religious wars, whose long-term effects can be observed well into the 20th century. The struggle was not between religion and tolerance, it was a struggle to make the state, religion and society coincide (*cuius regio, eius religio*). In essence, it is not secularism and tolerance that have shaped European political cultures, but wars of religion.

The 1648 Treaty of Westphalia established the modern nation state, which at first imposed the hegemonic role of a given religion. Secularism here just meant that the role of religion was defined by the political body, not that religion was pushed outside the public space. Until recently, freedom of religion in Europe meant freedom for religious minorities, more than an individual human right. These 'religious minorities' were dealt with under different paradigms: that of 'toleration', providing a lower status (Protestants in France in 1787, Catholics in Great Britain in 1827, Protestants in Spain in 1967 and, after the ban on minarets, Muslims in Switzerland) or of "protected minority under international treaties" (Alsatian Protestants in France after 1648, Crimean Tatars in Russia after 1787, Muslims in Greece under the Treaty of Lausanne in 1923). In some countries where no religion was dominant, equal legal recognition was bestowed upon a limited number of religious communities (Protestantism and Catholicism, in Germany and the Netherlands, for instance), but that does not mean equal treatment for any religion (Judaism is legally recognised as a religion in Germany, but not – yet – Islam). Therefore the difference between 'great' religions and 'religious minorities' is still at work even where no official religion is established.

Even the French *laïcité* does not consider all religions as equal although they are all supposed to belong to the private sphere: there is still a hierarchy of religions. The French Catholic Church has many privileges (churches built before 1905 are maintained by the local municipalities, official protocol puts the Catholic clergy in a higher position than other clergy in official ceremonies). Only four religions have the right to provide chaplains (Catholicism, Protestantism, Judaism and Islam[9]). And finally, the French Parliament has established a commission to curb 'cults', which means that the law was able to draw a line between 'religions' and 'cults' and thus define what a religion is. Religion is as much as ever a political issue.

Thus, far from being a history of slow and peaceful secularisation, relations between states and religions have always been conflictual in Europe and are a central part of European political cultures. This explains the fact that Europe has not just one, but several political cultures: there is little parallel between the definition of secularism in Germany, France and Italy, or between the role of the Catholic Church in Spain, Great Britain, Germany or the Netherlands.

The myth of Western values

The process of disentangling religion and culture among second generation Muslims in Europe is not acknowledged by the authorities, public opinion and media, but it is going on. In fact, proof of this 'autonomisation' of the religious factor is that the debate in most European countries is about religious symbols, not ethnic markers: veil, burqa, minarets, mosques and halal food. Nevertheless these religious markers are still often seen as 'cultural' markers, hence the permanent confusion. But this confusion is also the result of the ambivalent coalition that opposes the visibility of Islam in Europe. For much of the left, Europe is first of all secular. Modern values (democracy, individual freedom, freedom of religion, and more recently gender equality and sexual freedom) have been established against religion and more specifically of course against Christianity. The rise of Islam puts into question the curb that secularism has imposed on religion in general. Hence containing Islam in Europe is not a fight in defence of Christianity, but in defence of recently acquired freedoms: first, the separation of religion and politics; second, the new values of the sixties (which all revolve around sexuality and family), which have never been accepted by the Catholic Church or the evangelical Protestants.

On the other hand, many rightists oppose Islam because they consider that Europe is first of all a Christian land. Nevertheless, for most of them, Christianity has little to do with religious practices, it has to do with identity, not faith. Interestingly enough, many secularists are increasingly aligning them-selves with the agenda of the Christian right by defining Europe as culturally Christian. But the Christianity they defend is not a faith, it is an identity. Religious practice is decreasing in Europe and this may be why staunch secularists

---

[9] Although Buddhists and Orthodoxes have recently been contacted to provide chaplains for prisons.

can now defend a 'Christian identity', precisely because faith is no longer a challenge to a secularist world view.

When he was president, Nicolas Sarkozy, who praises the Catholic Church but never goes to church, opposed Turkey's accession to the European Union on these premises. This view is also endorsed by the Italian Northern League, which assaulted the Patriarch of Milan for his supposed support for migrants, while calling for the cross to be put on the Italian national flag.

Hence an apparently shared reluctance towards the rise of the visibility of Islam among at least three very different segments of European public opinion (secularists, the Christian right and the 'born again' of different faiths) conceals very different, even conflicting agendas. Islam is the negative identity of a Europe that is unable to forge a common – much less positive – identity for itself.

Interestingly enough, the 'pro-Islam' elements among European political activists share the same lack of understanding of the shift from cultural Islam to Islam as a universal religion: they tend to be found in a very secular ultra-left (like the former mayor of London, Ken Livingstone), which supports Muslims not as believers but as the 'imported' part of the Third World, embodying the intersection between the working class (or 'underclass' when they are out of the job market) and the Third World. These activists, by definition, ignore the purely religious dimension of Islam, and tend to stress its cultural and political dimension (for instance by supporting multiculturalism). They too miss the growing disconnect between religion and culture and, not so incidentally, the rise of a 'believing' Muslim middle class which tends to be conservative in terms of moral values and to align with conservative Christians.

In fact there is no consensus in Europe about common values: abortion, same-sex marriage, assisted procreation have become the real dividing lines between the active faith communities and the rest of society. Traditional believers, born-agains and converts are at the core of the faith communities and tend to identify with the surrounding culture less and less: for them Europe is no longer Christian. By contrast, secularists turned islamophobe do not find the way back to empty churches: for them Christianity has to do with identity, not faith. And conversely, many Christian and Jewish believers realise that Islam-bashing could turn into religion-bashing: in France for instance, the three main religious representative bodies (Catholic, Jewish and Protestant) did not support the ban of the veil for school children.

We can conclude here that the apparent polarisation between a European public opinion stressing Western values and a Muslim faith community is the result of an optical illusion. It hides the changing patterns of relationship between religion and culture and the in-depth reshuffle of the different paradigms that have stabilised the tensions between religion and politics in Europe. But it also hides the changing patterns of religiosity among Muslims in Europe. There is no longer any cultural evidence of Islam, and the religion transmitted by their parents to the Muslims that live in Europe today appears to them enmeshed in a culture they no longer share. They have to reconstruct what it means to be a Muslim.

The formatting of Islam in the West

In traditional Muslim societies, religious prescriptions are embedded in culture and often in law. In a situation in which Muslims are a minority, these prescriptions are disentangled from the web of socially acceptable and culturally normative attitudes: they have to be recast as purely religious norms. But they are also sorted differently and categorized according to the legal system of the host country: this will be referred to as the formatting effect of the state. The right to wear the veil, for instance, could be treated according to different co-existing normative domains: gender equality, personal freedom, neutrality of the civil service, labour laws, security requirements, etc. Religious norms are recast either as values or as new norms defined by new paradigms (individual freedom, freedom of religion). This formatting effect is not only accepted, but also promoted by Muslims (liberals as well as conservatives).

Muslims in Europe, like any religious minority, have no problem with the separation of church and state, because the state is not, and has no chance of becoming 'Islamic'. Throughout the history of the Muslim world, power has mostly been a very secular practice, even if the ruler had to give lip service to religion. For instance, theocracy was almost unknown until the Islamic revolution of Iran. The *ulama*, a professional guild of religious experts, were never in charge of political affairs: they did provide politicians, judges and civil servants with legitimacy of power, but were not themselves in charge of state power. In fact, the very rise of 'Islamist movements' in the mid-20th century (like the Muslim Brothers), who claimed that no existing Muslim country could be called an 'Islamic state', shows how the divide between religion and politics was acknowledged by the supporters of an Islamic state. Only a revolution could impose (and not restore) an Islamic state that had never existed, except (but even this is controversial) during the early period of the Islamic community. Islamic law, *sharia,* is not a closed legal code but is open to interpretation and adaptation by professional judges.

When sharia is transformed into the law of the state, it loses its authenticity because no state can give free rein to professional judges not just to implement the law but to 'make' the law outside the control of the state. State implementation of the sharia is either the end of the state (the Pakistani or Afghan Taliban) or the end of the sharia (Iran, where the learned clergy has been slowly but continuously disengaging itself from a dictatorship increasingly controlled by a lay apparatus based on the Revolutionary Guards).

But at least as far as Muslims in Europe are concerned, the main issue is not, once again, about "what does Islam really say?" but what their real religious practices are. The point missed by the Western debate is how Muslims, including activists, are transformed by their interaction with Western secular society, without neglecting the fact that this society is also transformed by a process of integration that forces it to rethink its traditional paradigms of national identity, challenged not only by immigration, but more deeply by the crisis of the modern nation state. It is interesting to note that the construction of the European Union is almost parallel with the timing of immigration. Immigration and European integration started around the same time (the fifties and sixties), in France the first debate on the veil (1989) came just before the debate on the Maastricht Treaty (1992), and the second crisis (leading to the law banning the veil in schools in 2004) happened just before the rejection of the Nice Treaty in France (2005). Thus, the nation state is challenged at the same time from above (Brussels) and from below (immigration), leading to a nationalist and populist backlash, often opposed both to Europe and to Islam.

In the mind of the European public opinion, sharia is the deterrent *par excellence*: Muslims are called upon to repudiate it, as President Sarkozy asked them to do in a famous television debate with Tariq Ramadan.[10] Ramadan's answer, which has been referred to as an example of his 'double speak', was that, while the sacred text cannot be changed, a moratorium on some of its implications should be announced. This position is in fact perfectly coherent with the two-world theory: there is the sacred space of religion and there is the society in which the believer is living and to which s/he should adapt. The secular state has nothing to say about the hereafter, and takes into consideration only worldly practices. Hence, for Muslims, the issue is not so much rejecting sharia as recasting it.

There are many ways to deal with sharia. The liberal one is to explain it in terms of values not norms, the way Reform Jews did in the 19th century. Petty and unacceptable norms are rejected because they were more or less adapted to a given society which no longer exists; the believer has to go back to the intention beyond the written norms and find a way to maintain the spirit of the law in a new context (for instance stressing decency instead of wearing a veil).

Moreover, a secular state will of course not implement punishments that could be advocated by some sharia norms. By acknowledging the impossibility of coercion, liberals as well as fundamentalists have to redefine sanctions in this profane world either as purely spiritual, or as based on contractual acceptance of arbitration courts which, by definition, are bound by the laws of the state. The demand to establish sharia courts in Canada and Great Britain has to be understood in this

---

[10] French channel Antenne 2, 20 November 2003.

context, where there is no question of introducing stoning or amputation. Even what is seen as the peak of the 'Islamisation' of Europe, the establishment of an arbitration sharia court, is also a way to format sharia in line with an existing judicial paradigm, an arbitration court that contracting parties agree to take as a referee. By the way, this explains why the call to grant legal recognition to sharia courts takes place only in common law countries, and not in continental Europe, where it cannot fit with the existing legal institutions.

Even 'non-liberal' views of sharia can lead to the disentanglement of religious norms and social behaviours, for example, by putting a religious marker on a secular social practice (halal fast food). The use of the headscarf is increasing among educated, second generation Muslim women, but their social practices are integrative, through education and access to the labour market: there are now headscarf-wearing executive women, and headscarf-wearing single mothers.

Sharia is for instance recast by Salafis as a personal handbook of precise norms, disconnected from their social context (because they consider this context as pagan even in traditional Muslim societies): how to dress, eat, wash, speak, etc. They use handbooks listing the norms that should direct the life of an individual Muslim in any circumstances, like *The Way of the Muslim* by Sheikh Aldjazairi.[11] But in the same book there is a chapter on "how to behave with slaves", which might seem rather irrelevant for converts and born-agains in destitute neighbourhoods of Paris suburbs. It is all the more disconcerting that Sheikh Aldjazairi does not advocate the establishment of an Islamic state, where slavery would be authorized, but writes as if slavery is a permanent pattern of society. Instead of double speak, such an attitude shows how disconnected the Salafi discourse is from real social and political issues. It corresponds more to a cult attitude, the withdrawal of unhappy believers into a closed and marginal faith community.

By trying to recast sharia as a normative system that does not rely on the state for implementation, most Muslims tend to transform it into an *à la carte* menu, depending on individual decisions or the advice of a more or less independent 'sheikh'. The same individual can freely shift from one interpretation to another, from one group to another, according to his or her individual trajectory. Whatever the choice between stressing values instead of norms or norms instead of spirit, the endeavour to develop sharia outside the scope of the state is a way to acknowledge secularisation: it also fits with the concept of the separation of church and state. A fundamentalist faith community can thrive in a secular and permissive society.

---

[11] A. Aldjazairi, *Minhaj ul Muslim* (*ebook*) http://ebookbrowse.com/minhaj-al-muslim-shiekh-abu-bakr-jaabir-al-jazairy-pdf-d186925065) translated into many European languages; the French version, *La voie du musulman* (there are different translations and publishers, and the spelling of the author's name might vary) is very popular and can be found in any Islamic bookshop in France.

The ambivalence of the secular state: providing freedom, controlling freedom

While the secular state, whatever its temptations, cannot reform a religion, it can play an important role in formatting it. The alternate stress on support (in the name of religious freedom) and restriction (in the name of public order), even if it is not based on a long-term coherent vision, has the effect of defining the conditions of practices, both negatively (restrictions on veil, processions, bell-ringing, call to prayers) and positively (giving official recognition to places of worship, appointing chaplains, granting tax exemption). This formatting is not restricted to government edicts and laws, it is also a consequence of court decisions, as well as of polemics and pressure from public opinion, often amplified by the media.

The process of formatting begins by granting a faith community the qualification of religion (hence admitting that the until that time dominant religions do not have a monopoly on truth and the sacred). It pushes a faith community to organise itself along the dominant paradigm. For example, imams are now expected to represents the community – which they do not do in traditional Islam – as priests or rabbis do. It re-organises the connections between norms and their theological background by making a distinction between 'high religion' (the essential tenets) and 'low religion' (cultural or surrogatory ones): for instance, by defining the burqa either as an expression of faith or, on the contrary, as having little to do with faith. It thus contributes to redefining Islam as a 'mere' religion. Marriage is a typical example of formatting: when a Muslim couple living in the West marries in a mosque, bride and groom hand in hand, the bride dressed in white and carrying a bouquet as in a Christian church wedding, is this merely a superficial adaptation, a change in the conception of the couple or is it a redefinition of the religious value of Muslim marriage?[12]

In fact, formatting is very often a process of interaction, reciprocal adjustments and reformulation of norms from very different cultural fields into a new set of norms aimed, if not at creating a consensus, at least at making the different norms and beliefs compatible and acceptable. Consensus is an ideal that often harks back to a mythical past, purportedly the casualty of some historical event that is deliberately evoked. Take, for example, the insistence in France on 'republican consensus' or 'republican norms', which are allegedly under threat from the arrival of Islam, whereas neither corresponds to historical fact: France has effectively been a republic since 1789, but against a permanent political backdrop of undeclared civil war, in which revolutionaries and reactionaries, the secular elites and clerics, communists and anti-communists continually brand their adversaries 'enemies of the nation'. This fantasy consensus is not the legacy of the good old days (that never were): it is the prospect on which the formatting of Islam is focused.

---

[12] Boubekeur, *Le voile de la mariée.*

One religion among others

The consequence of this formatting, both through the personal practices of the believers and through state pressure and action, is to put Islam within the same paradigm as the other religions. What is the new shared 'format' that Islam is now increasingly sharing with the other religions in the West? There are three dimensions to it:

A convergence of religiosities, in other words, defining faith and the believer's relationship to his/her religion, often expressed in terms of a spiritual quest. The market offers a range of products to fulfil one and the same demand. This demand thus tends to be standardised by the market, reflecting the consumers' image of what it is supposed to be. Nowadays, religion is no longer defined by anthropologists or philosophers, and less and less by the "professionals" – clerics or preachers – chasing after the convert/customer. Individual conversions often illustrate this itinerant, nomadic, even eclectic characteristic of the new believer.

A convergence of definitions: the notion of 'religion' becomes a normative paradigm with no specific content. It is the designation of any system as a religion, without taking account of the content that makes it a religion: these days, it is the courts that decide in the event of a dispute, even though they claim not to deal with matters of theology. Even, and perhaps especially, in countries where there is a strict division between religion and power (France, the United States) which prohibits the state from defining what a religion is, it is still necessary to specify who or what is entitled to the label of a 'religion', even if only to allow for religious freedom (exemption from tax, chaplaincy, definition of places of worship, dietary exemptions, religious holidays, etc.). Democratisation and human rights theory tend to standardise the definition of religion (like that of a minority), in order to treat everyone equally. Secularism thus creates religion since, in order to keep it at a distance, it must assign religion a place and therefore define it as a 'pure religion'.[13] Formatting also aims to standardise the manifestation of religion in the public sphere: 'religious practice' is thus overseen, from the wearing of the headscarf by Muslim women to the erection of an *eruv* (a thread that turns a neighbourhood into a private sphere for Shabbat) around an orthodox Jewish neighbourhood, or the right to smoke hashish (a demand by the Rastafarians in the United States, which was rejected) or to drink wine (during mass in prohibitionist countries) as part of religious practice.

An institutional convergence among religions: the figure of the 'priest' or the 'minister' tends to define all religious practitioners or professionals (many Western armed forces have already appointed 'Muslim chaplains', something that does not exist in most Muslim armies); *ulama* (religious scholars) become theologians, imams and rabbis become 'parish' leaders. In the name of equality between

---

[13] See Roy, *Secularism Confronts Islam*.

believers, the law, courts and also institutions tend to format all religions in the same way. For example, in extending the principle of chaplaincy to Islam, the army and the prison authorities reinforce the institutional alignment of Islam with Christianity. In this sense we can speak of the 'churchification' of religions by courts and states.

Thus, the real issue is not an intellectual or theoretical question about Islam, but the religious practices of Muslims. The forms of religiosity in Islam today are more or less the same as those found in Catholicism, Protestantism, and even Judaism. Contemporary adherents insist more on personal faith and individual spiritual experience. Such 'born again' believers rebuild their identities from the perspective of their rediscovery of religion.

Islam does not bring a new culture or new values, but is the mirror through which Europe is looking at its own identity. The emergence of Islam in Europe is part of a general reshuffling of the religious landscape and of a new relationship between faith communities, states and societies. Forms of Islam can be found across the whole spectrum of religious attitudes (from liberal to fundamentalist). Indeed, all forms of religious fundamentalism rely on the notion of a 'pure' religion, independent of cultural variations and influences. Today's Islamic revival shares the dogmatism, communitarism, and scripturalism of American evangelist movements: both reject culture, philosophy and even theology in favour of a literalist reading of the sacred texts and an immediate understanding of truth through individual faith.[14]

Conclusion

Fundamentalist or conservative forms of religion are more in tune with the present process of globalisation and deculturation. This does not mean that fundamentalism is the future of religion. Traditional Christian churches are desperately trying to reconnect with an increasingly secular society, and they will have to find a more open discourse. The social integration of Muslims is leading to the rise of new forms of religiosity that will soon or later produce their own theological updating. But in the meantime public authorities should adopt a clear policy, coherent with both political (separation of state and religion) and social secularism (religion is not at the core of the social bond). Islam should be addressed as a religion in the framework of the national 'pacts' managing the role of religions in the public sphere: *laïcité* in France, majority-minority in Italy, official status in Austria, etc. Multiculturalism is a dead end because it ignores the specificity of the religious dimension in favour of an ill-defined 'identity'. Cultural issues (language, ethnicity) should be separated from religious issues: if Islam was an ethnic religion for

---

[14] Roy, *Holy Ignorance.*

the first generation, conversions (in both directions) and the rise of new generations entails an increasing disconnect between the two. And finally, instead of parroting the populists, politicians should clearly address the issue of the so-called Christian identity of Europe: the more one claims this identity, the less one goes to church. Even if the identity of Europe is Christian, it is no longer a religious identity because faith has left. That is exactly the message that the Popes have been repeating for the last 25 years – and they know best.

Nostalgia is not a policy: the issue now is to set out what European values are, and no doubt most of the faithful will be able to share them.

References

Ben Cheykh, S. *Marianne, le Prophète*. Paris: Grasset, 1998.

Boubekeur, A. *Le voile de la mariée: Jeunes musulmanes, voile et, projet matrimonial en France*. Paris: L'Harmattan, 2004.

Manji, I. *The Trouble With Islam Today: A Muslim's Call for Reform in Her Faith*. New York: Saint Martin's Griffin, 2005.

Rajab, T. *Re-Programming British Muslims – A Study of the Islam Channel*. London: Quilliam Foundation, March 2010.

Roy, O. *Holy Ignorance*. New York: Columbia University Press, 2010.

Roy, O. *Secularism Confronts Islam*. New York: Columbia University Press, 2007.

Sageman, M. *Understanding Terrorist Networks*. Philadelphia: Philadelphia University Press, 2004.

EU Foreign Policy and Political Islam: Towards a New Entente in the Post-Arab Spring Era?

Timo Behr

The rise of political Islam in the EU's southern neighbourhood represents a political as well as conceptual challenge to the EU as a foreign policy actor. In the past, the EU reacted to this challenge based on its essentialist perception of political Islam and its overarching interest in regional stability and security. However, the growing salience of 'contingencist' interpretations of political Islam and the resolution of the EU's democratisation-stabilisation dilemma in the wake of the Arab Spring have recently provided an opportunity for greater engagement and cooperation. This has enabled a switch in EU policies from a strategy of containment to a strategy of engagement. Despite this, problems remain as the EU continues to expect Islamist actors to adjust to its own discursive framework and as intra-European divisions revive as a result of the renewal of secular-religious divisions in the neighbourhood. This will complicate EU attempts to build a new partnership with Islamist democracies and will fuel old stereotypes and animosities.

The triumph of Islamist parties in a string of post 'Arab Spring' elections from Morocco to Egypt has been greeted with mixed feeling in European capitals. While some have welcomed them as confirmation that Islam and democracy are compatible, others remain squeamish about the impact of an 'Islamist winter' on individual liberties and regional stability in the neighbourhood. As a foreign policy actor, the EU has always faced a dilemma when dealing with Islamist movements and actors. Divisions in EU foreign policy concerning Islamism have often been just as bitter as divisions about the role of Islam in domestic politics, and not infrequently these two have come to reflect on each other, as with French fears over the domestic impact of the Algerian civil war or with the anti-Islamic policies of the Dutch Freedom Party.

Partly as a result of this close connection between domestic debates about Islam and EU foreign policy debates about Islamism, the EU's interactions with Islamist actors in its neighbourhood have often been difficult and erratic. While the EU has never adopted an explicit collective policy towards Islamist movements, its policies, statements and regional initiatives suggest an implicit approach shaped by European perceptions and interests. This approach has not only changed significantly over time and space – between various episodes of benign neglect, cautious engagement and overt hostility – but has also been one of the key elements determining the EU's collective policies in the neighbourhood. Despite this, few attempts have been made to understand how European views of Islam have affected its collective foreign policy in the neighbourhood.

EU foreign policy and political Islam

To understand what drives the EU's approach towards Islamist movements in its southern neighbourhood requires, first of all, a better understanding of the nature and aims of EU foreign policy. Over the years, the EU's role as a foreign policy actor in the Mediterranean has been closely scrutinized in the academic literature. Particularly close attention has generally been paid to the EU's role as both a 'value promoter' and 'region-builder' in the Mediterranean, two issues that have often been seen as intrinsically linked.[1] Much of the literature on EU foreign affairs has ascribed the special attention that the EU has devoted to these issues as deriving from the EU's assumed normative nature as a foreign policy actor.[2]

The starting point for this literature is the 'normative power' Europe paradigm, according to which the EU is a unique international actor that has been founded on a collective identity, drawing on a shared set of common liberal democratic norms and values. While these norms define the EU's internal structure and policies, they have also come to shape its relations with the outside world. The EU, in other words, acts more as a constructivist norms exporter than as a realist power projector.[3] Being neither able nor willing to employ power politics, the EU has turned into a post-modern state whose fundamental foreign policy aim is to extend its post-modern bubble – above all to its crisis-ridden Mediterranean neighbours.[4] According to this argument, the EU's interaction with the Mediterranean countries is primarily driven by the EU's urge to extend and replicate its liberal-democratic discourse in its relations with its neighbours.

---

[1] Adler, *The Convergence of Civilizations*.
[2] Manners, "Normative Power Europe".
[3] Pace, "The Construction of EU Normative Power".
[4] Cooper, *The Breaking of Nations*.

Over time, however, some critical voices have questioned this normative tradition in EU foreign policy analysis. According to these authors, the EU does not possess a specific nature or ethos and is quite capable of pursuing its realist foreign policy interests in a rational manner.[5] Evidence for this can be found in the EU's conduct in the Mediterranean. Not only has the EU's democracy discourse proven to be devoid of content in the Mediterranean context, but EU foreign policy also continues to be driven by the member states, not the EU's common institutions.[6] In a much quoted article, Adrian Hyde-Prize concluded that "Europe's great powers will continue to jealously guard their sovereign rights to pursue their own foreign and security priorities."[7] In the Mediterranean this has meant that EU policies have tended to favour stability over democracy.

Most recently, a number of authors have argued against an 'either-or' approach in EU foreign policy analysis and in favour of a more flexible conceptualization of the EU as an actor that captures the combined impact of interests and values. While these authors argue that norms continue to matter, they seek to move beyond the normative framework imposed by the 'normative power Europe' paradigm and accept the role of national interests.[8] This suggests a more flexible EU foreign policy outlook that is able to adjust both aims and methods. In the words of Björn Hettne and Fredrik Söderbaum, EU policies "will vary between true civilianism and soft imperialism. Behind these two ideal-type positions lie various combinations or norms and (material and other) interests."[9]

Accepting the post-normative turn in EU foreign policy analysis suggests that the EU acts neither as a shrewd defender of regional stability, nor as a starry-eyed promoter of liberal democracy. Rather EU foreign policy represents a sliding scale between those two poles that is able to adjust flexibly and pragmatically to its perception of regional developments and actors and the way they relate to the EU's own interests and values. This suggests that when and where the EU *perceives* political Islam to be in conflict with its own interests and values, it has opted to disengage. Similarly, in the absence of such a perceived conflict with political Islam, a more open attitude towards engagement and cooperation can reasonably be expected.

This shifts the focus towards how and why the EU might perceive that its interests and identity in the neighbourhood could be threatened by political Islam. In order to do so, it is necessary to revisit the never-ending essentialist-contingencist debate about Islam and democracy and how it has informed EU foreign policy.[10] Arguably, the dispute between essentialist and contingencist

---

[5] Cavatorta and Pace, "The Post-Normative Turn", 592.
[6] Behr, "Enduring Differences?"
[7] Hyde-Prize, *European Security in the Twenty First Century,* 113.
[8] Seeberg, "European Neighbourhood Policy".
[9] Hettne and Söderbaum, "Civilian Power or Soft Imperialism?", 551.
[10] Hurd, "Political Islam and Foreign Policy".

interpretations of political Islam has been at the heart of the EU's debate on the relationship of Islam to democracy and provides a core element to the argument that Western relations with Islam have become 'securitized' after 9/11.

Cultural essentialists, such as Bernard Lewis and Samuel Huntington, have famously argued that Islamic traditions and scripture are incompatible with Western-style democracy and that political Islam remains a throttle on the development of a liberal democratic culture.[11] This claim is based on the assertion that distinctions between religious and political authority, which according to secular epistemology are a fundamental precondition for Western liberal democratic modernity, are entirely absent from the agenda of political Islam.[12] According to the French scholar Gilles Kepel, the "separation of the secular and religious domains is the prerequisite for liberating the forces of reform in the Muslim world".[13] Based on this, essentialists deny that it is possible to distinguish between 'moderate' and 'radical' forms of political Islam or that engagement with Islamist parties can lead to any form of democratic socialisation.

This essentialist view has been challenged by a number of contingencists who reject reductionist interpretations of political Islam and, on the contrary, stress its potential to serve as a vanguard of Middle Eastern democracy.[14] They have done so by arguing that essentialism "rides roughshod over the diversity of views and experiences of contention among Muslims".[15] According to François Burgat, Islamists' terms of reference, modes of expression and behaviour are more the product of a specific domestic and international context than universal Islamist principles and are therefore likely to change in accordance with this context.[16] While there is some disagreement amongst contingencists on whether dialogue and inclusion leads to a superficial moderation of Islamist strategies and tactics or might have a deeper impact on their core values and beliefs, they agree that the political context remains the prime variable determining their behaviour and outlook.[17]

This article argues that the EU's foreign policies towards Islamist parties and organisations in its neighbourhood can be explained by combining the EU's collective 'views' of political Islam (as defined by the essentialist-contingencist debate) with the EU's policy 'goals' in the Mediterranean (as defined by the constructivist-realist debate). The resulting matrix provides four different modes of interaction between the EU and political Islam that are defined by the different views/goals

---

[11] Lewis, *What Went Wrong?*; Tibi, "Why They Can't Be Democratic".
[12] Hurd, "Political Islam and Foreign Policy".
[13] Kepel, *The War for Muslim Minds*, 295
[14] For example, Halliday, *Islam and the Myth of Confrontation*, and Eposito, "The Islamic Threat".
[15] Wedeen, "Beyond the Crusades", 1.
[16] Burgat, *Face to Face with Political Islam*.
[17] For contrasting views, see Wickham, "The Path to Moderation", and Schwedler "Democratization, Inclusion and the Moderation of Islamist Parties".

adopted by the EU. The following section argues that the EU's mix of views/goals has changed considerably over time, as a result of three significant events and their interpretation in Europe – the Algerian Civil War, 9/11 and the Arab Spring – leading to an adjustment of EU policies.

View/Goal	Norms-Entrepreneur	Stability-Promoter
Essentialist	Oppose	Contain
Contingencist	Engage	Differentiate

Change and continuity in EU-Islam relations

The Algerian civil war: containing the rise of Islam

The question of how to deal with the new phenomenon of political Islam imposed itself on Europe for the first time during the late 1980s. The Iranian revolution, the fatwa against Salman Rushdie, the French *affaire du foulard* and the first Palestinian *Intifada*, all drew attention to the rising power and influence of political Islam, following the decline of Arab nationalism in the Middle East.[18] However, it was the Algerian civil war in particular that shaped the prism through which the EU perceived the region. According to Amel Boubekeur and Samir Amghar, "in the 1990s, European policymakers did not equate Islamist movements with institutionalized political parties, but rather with the attacks in the Paris underground or the hijacking of the Air France aircraft".[19]

As a result, there was a tendency to characterise political Islam as being one of a number of 'new security threats' that the EU was facing in its neighbourhood at the time, alongside issues such as mass migration, international crime, transnational terrorism and economic instability. This hostile and largely essentialist view of Islamist movements as a security threat was reinforced by other events in the region. In Palestine, it was Hamas' opposition to the Oslo Peace Process and its indiscriminate use of suicide bombers in the mid-1990s that threatened peace and stability. In Egypt, it was the bloody terrorist campaign of the *Al-Gama'a al-Islamiyya* that shocked and repelled Western observers.

The resulting essentialist image of a monolithic and hostile Islamist challenge combined with a strong European focus on stability in its southern neighbourhood. Throughout the 1980s, Western strategy in general had become preoccupied with the image of an 'arc of crisis' in the Middle East, given fears of a regional domino effect following the Iranian revolution.[20] Moreover, at a time when a number of

---

[18] Ajami, *Dream Palace of the Arabs*.
[19] Boubekeur and Amghar, *Islamist Parties in the Maghreb*.
[20] Spencer, "Algeria: France's Disarray", 175.

Central and Eastern European countries managed a successful transition towards democracy, Algeria's failure appeared to suggest that the Middle East was not yet ready for political change. This meant that European countries favoured a more gradual path for the region that sought to prevent spillover from the Algerian crisis and the containment of hostile Islamist movements. Faced with what has often been aptly described as the democratisation-stabilisation dilemma, Europe opted for the autocratic stability that most served its interests.[21]

Within the EU, France acted as one of the main advocates of this policy of containment. Conscious of the price of regional instability and worried about the impact of Islamist movements on its own Muslim population, France considered Muslim *intégrisme* as a double challenge for its foreign policy and domestic cohesion.[22] Given France's dominance of the Euro-Med portfolio this inevitably shaped EU policies.

Although the EU continued to emphasize mutual dialogue, respect for human rights and greater political freedoms in its public diplomacy, the implicit approach that it developed *vis-à-vis* the new Islamist actors in the region was one of containment. This containment approach became evident at several levels. In the case of the Algerian civil war, the EU's inaction and silence, as well as its economic support, amounted to siding with the Algerian military. The EU's only attempt at mediation, the 1998 Troika mission, ended in failure and, according to Jünemann, "left the impression of unreserved EU support for the Algerian regime and its strategy of ending the civil war by force alone".[23]

Similarly, the Euro-Mediterranean Partnership launched in 1995, largely as an answer to the growing instability in the EU's southern neighbourhood and as a sign of the EU's growing self-confidence as an international actor, endorsed the regional status quo. Although democracy promotion and a bottom-up civil society dialogue was part of the EMP's agenda, they were implemented in a way that they excluded any real dialogue with Islamist parties and organisations.[24] Moreover, cognizant of its reliance on authoritarian Arab governments as partners in the process of building a Eurocentric Mediterranean region, the EU flinched from using the conditionality clauses that were enshrined in the Barcelona Declaration in order to press for political reforms.

Instead, the EU policies focused on reviving economic growth and development in order to address the "root problems" of violence and to ensure some measure of regional stability. Conveniently, economic development was also seen as the best way to counteract the pressure of illegal migration to Europe – one of the main

---

[21] Behr, "Enduring Differences?"
[22] Chevènement, *Le vert et le noir.*
[23] Jünemann, "Support for Democracy".
[24] Johansson-Nogués, *Civil Society in Euro-Mediterranean Relations.*

concerns for especially the southern European countries.[25] Finally, the EU sub-scribed to the common neo classical view that with time economic liberalisation would facilitate a political opening. To limit the potential for violent friction and turmoil, the EU argued that reforms had to be 'sequenced' with economic reforms preceding democratisation.[26] Middle Eastern societies first had to be 'fit' for democracy which would only come when the foundation of a moderate, secular society that excluded Islamist parties had been laid.

The global war on terror: dividing friend from foe

The terrorist attacks of 9/11 profoundly changed the global political climate, forcing the EU to revisit its approach to political Islam. Worried that the virulent US reaction to the attacks might trigger a 'clash of civilisations', the EU's initial response was to try and deflate religious tensions by calling for more dialogue. In the immediate aftermath of 9/11 this resulted in a number of EU statements emphasizing that Islam was not the enemy and endorsing greater cultural exchanges.[27] As Romano Prodi stated after the 9/11 attacks: "We must avoid at all costs the association between terrorism and the Arab and Islamic world. We are engaged in a dialogue between equals and we should promote this through cultural exchange. It is of utmost importance that we continue our dialogue."[28]

EU fears of a looming clash of civilisations were further heightened as a result of the terrorist attacks in Madrid and London. Political Islam, as a result, ceased to be a mere foreign policy issue and became part of the EU's domestic agenda. While this led to some 'securitization' of Islam more generally, it also inspired numerous attempts at dialogue and engagement with Islamic actors and organisations in EU member states, as well as in EU foreign policy. Initiatives such as the Turkish-Spanish Alliance of Civilisations and the EU's Anna Lindh Foundation proliferated throughout the 2000s, providing the basis for a much more differentiated and contingencist view of political Islam. These in many ways represented the flip-side to the various Islam Conferences and dialogue initiatives at the domestic level as European countries began to grapple with the challenge of diversity.

The transformation of political Islam in Turkey and the reformist policy agenda adopted by the Justice and Development Party (AKP) following Turkey's 2002 general elections, seemed to confirm a more benign view of political Islam. A number of other moderate Islamist parties in the region soon attempted to emulate the AKP's success and began to visibly moderate their agendas. While most analysts now accepted that the "outcome of participation [of Islamist parties]

---

[25] Joffé, "The European Union, Democracy and Counter-Terrorism".
[26] Kienle, "Political Reform through Economic Reform?"
[27] Silvestri, "Islam and Religion".
[28] European Commission, "President Prodi Participation".

is not invariably a process of further democratization and moderation, it is also clear that non-participation (...) is a guarantee that a process of moderation will not take place".[29] The result was an increasing trend within the EU and elsewhere not only to adopt a more contingencist view of Islam, but also to consider democratisation more seriously as a long-term foreign policy goal in the region.

Ironically, one of the main motivations for the EU to modify its rigid focus on stability in the neighbourhood was the US Freedom Agenda in the Middle East. Based on an assumed link between the lack of democracy and the rise of terrorism in the Middle East, the Bush administration made an effort to engage a number of Islamist actors that it deemed 'moderate'.[30] The concrete results of this policy were twofold: First, US pressure led to a brief democratic opening in the mid-2000s, as Middle Eastern governments allowed a greater measure of electoral competition and eased restrictions on freedom of speech. Second, the US gradually developed contacts with some moderate Islamist movements in Morocco, Yemen and Jordan.[31] The EU soon followed suit by developing its own channels of communication with some of these Islamist actors.

Evidence for this new approach can be found in various EU documents at the time. Thus, the EU Strategic Partnership with the Mediterranean and Middle East in 2004 called for an EU engagement "with non-violent political organisations and civil society movements at all levels in society, with such engagement open to all organisations committed to non-violent and democratic means".[32] Even more explicit was the EU's Strategy on Combating Radicalisation and Recruitment to Terrorism in 2005, stating that "we need to empower moderate voices by engaging with Muslim organisations and faith groups that reject the distorted version of Islam put forward by al-Qa'ida and others... . We must ensure that by our own policies we do not exacerbate divisions."[33]

The result was a differentiated approach under which the EU increasingly moved away from a monolithic and essentialist view of political Islam and began to distinguish between 'moderates' and 'radicals'. Pressure to adopt a new approach in the region culminated in 2005–06, but ultimately failed. An EU foreign ministers meeting in 2005 considered the potential to engage with a wider range of faith-based groups in the Middle East, but did not initiate any concrete actions.[34] Following the surprise election victory of Hamas in 2006, the European Commission once more took the lead by establishing a Task Force on Political Islam within the Directorate General for External Relations. The Task Force drafted a discussion paper that outlined a set of common principles and conditions

---

[29] Ottaway and Hamzawy, *Islamists in Politics*.
[30] Amirah-Fernández and Menéndez, "Reform in Comparative Perspective".
[31] Yacoubian, *Engaging Islamists and Promoting Democracy*.
[32] European Council, *EU Strategic Partnership*, 8.
[33] European Council, *EU Strategy for Combating Radicalisation*, 4.
[34] Emerson and Youngs, *Political Islam and European Foreign Policy*.

that could serve as the basis for a more comprehensive European approach towards political Islam, but was ultimately blocked by the EU member states.[35]

Behind this failure were divergent visions in the EU member states of the role and nature of political Islam. Thus while some member states, such as Germany and the UK, had initiated explicit dialogue initiatives with Islamist actors in the early 2000s, others, like France and the Netherlands, remained sceptical about the prospects of engagement.[36] Scepticism was boosted by regional developments in the mid-2000s.

Following a strong showing of the Muslim Brotherhood in the 2005 Egyptian elections and the victory of Hamas in the 2006 elections, US and European concerns over the potential impact of these actors on regional stability halted the progress towards a more open approach. While contacts continued at a low level between the EU and moderate Islamist MPs in a number of Arab countries, EU pressure for political reforms effectively died away in the aftermath of the Hamas victory. This contributed to a progressive erosion and suspension of the EU's normative agenda in the region, with European policies being increasingly directed at business development and security cooperation. The shift from the Commission-centred Barcelona Process to the intergovernmental Union for the Mediterranean (UfM) became emblematic of this process.[37]

The Arab Spring: moderation through engagement?

The Arab Spring uprisings of early 2011 represent a watershed in the EU's relationship with political Islam. Initially, Europeans reacted in line with their preference for stability and security in the neighbourhood. As a result, the EU largely ignored the Tunisian uprising until the very last moment, while some of its member states, most notably France and Italy, sought to undermine a common position that could unseat a long-time ally. However, once Ben Ali was toppled and protests took on the hallmark of a region-wide democracy movement, the EU recovered its footing. During the Tahrir Square protests in Egypt, the EU followed the US lead in calling for a peaceful and inclusive democratic transition process. In Libya, Europeans sided even more forcefully with the protesters, despite some initial hesitations and internal disagreements.

As a result of these events, the EU embarked on a sweeping change of its policies. In a series of statements and public declarations from February 2011 onwards, various EU representatives argued that the region was now 'fit for democracy' and that it was the duty of the EU to side with the young revolutionaries

---

[35] Kausch, "Europe's Engagement with Moderate Islamists".
[36] In 2002, Germany initiated a mainly culturally-oriented dialogue with the Islamic world initiative, while the UK launched the Engaging with the Islamic World Group (EIWG) in 2004.
[37] Behr, *Regional Integration in the Mediterranean*.

struggling for freedom. From the EU's perspective this was rational.[38] Once governments had been toppled, it was in the best interest of the EU to assist a speedy transition towards a new democratic stability. In order to assist this transition and bolster its standing with the new leaders of the region, in March 2011 the EU adopted a new Partnership for Democracy and Shared Prosperity with the southern Mediterranean, which turned democracy promotion into a central goal of the EU's policy and promised greater EU aid and assistance.[39]

At the EU level, the result of the Arab Spring revolutions was therefore to resolve the inherent dichotomy between democracy and stability that had had such a firm hold on EU policies since the Algerian civil war. Instead of seeing these as opposed, the EU now acknowledged that 'sustainable stability' required democratic governance.[40]

At the same time, the EU also continued to express a largely contingencist view of political Islam, despite some divisions amongst its ranks. Thus, the EU was quick to acknowledge that any future political process needed to be 'inclusive' and include major Islamist parties like the Muslim Brotherhood. Given the relative restraint that Islamists displayed during these revolutions, few expected them to play a dominant political role in the future, thus lessening intra-European tensions over adopting a more inclusive approach. This meant that as *Ennahda* and the Muslim Brotherhood registered to compete in the polls, the EU sought to engage them more directly in political dialogue and High Representative Catherine Ashton and other European foreign ministers met repeatedly with their representatives while visiting the region. No longer able to ignore the Islamists, the EU now opted for a strategy of moderation through engagement.

However, the strong performance of Islamist parties in the post-revolutionary polls in Egypt and Tunisia, as well as the emergence of a vocal Salafist opposition, once again caught the EU by surprise and presented it with a new dilemma. According to one analyst, the dilemma is "how to deal with Islamism as a legitimate political power in the region without denying the EU's commitment to liberal norms and values, defended by their traditional partners in the liberal and secular spectrum of Arab civil society?"[41] To this could be added another dimension, namely: how to bind Islamist actors to a regional order that they perceive as inherently oppressive and hostile to their interests? Here, new differences are emerging between EU countries, with some demanding more direct support for liberal and progressive forces, while others urge caution and cooperation.

---

[38] J. M. Barroso, "Partners in Freedom: the EU Response to the Arab Spring", speech at the Opera House Cairo, Egypt, 14 July 2011.
[39] Behr, *The EU and the Arab Transition.*
[40] Behr, "The EU and Arab Democracy".
[41] Jünemann, *Civil Society, its Role and Potential.*

The EU has pursued a compromise approach that emphasizes the promotion of liberal values and an inclusive political process. According to Catherine Ashton, the EU wants to support the establishment of "deep democracy: not just organizing one election, but building institutions and ensuring people's rights – freedom of expression, freedom of religion and respect for minorities".[42] The EU has used this emphasis on inclusiveness to try to influence domestic processes. For example, by emphasizing its support for an 'inclusive and transparent solution' to Egypt's constitutional crisis, the EU tried to ensure the inclusion of liberal actors into Egypt's Constitutional Assembly.

Similarly, the EU has placed a strong emphasis on specific issues, such as women's rights or Egypt's peace treaty with Israel, and has sought reassurances from the new Islamist actors on these issues. It has done so by consistently emphasizing these issues as a precondition for good relations. Thus, when congratulating Mohammed Morsi on his election as Egyptian President, Catherine Ashton announced a large increase in EU funding for women's projects and stressed the importance of minority rights.[43]

The other way in which the EU has sought to influence the establishment of post-Arab Spring regimes has been by endorsing, and actively supporting, particular transitional actors. In the case of Libya, the EU's support for the National Transitional Council (NTC) and its leadership undoubtedly played a role in empowering liberal expatriates. Similarly, in Syria, the EU has tried hard to provide a leading role for liberals and moderate Islamists in the Syrian opposition. Finally, the EU has thrown its unmitigated support behind the questionable reform programs adopted by the Moroccan and Jordanian monarchs and has refrained from engaging more widely with opposition actors of different strains in those countries.[44]

The EU, in other words, can be seen as having pursued a two-pronged approach following the Arab Spring. On the one hand, the emphasis has been on moderation through engagement in those countries where Islamist political actors have established themselves as the dominant force. On the other hand, the EU has sought to check the dominance of Islamists by supporting those actors that appear closest to its own position, whether they be the Moroccan King, liberals in the Syrian opposition, or women's groups in Egypt.

The EU also increasingly acknowledges the diverse nature of political Islam and has sought to differentiate between different types of organisations. Thus, the EU has developed close ties with Ennahda, but remains guarded vis-à-vis the Muslim Brotherhood and has sought to contain the more conservative Salafist parties. While the EU has come a long way in reshaping its approach towards political

---

[42] European Commission, "Remarks by High Representative".
[43] *Ibid.*
[44] Entelis, *Morocco's New Political Face.*

Islam since the 1990s, the relationship is still characterised by a lack of trust and problems will continue as the EU struggles to adjust to an unfamiliar new partner.

Conclusion

EU relations with political Islam have come a long way over the least two decades, as member states adjusted their perceptions of political Islam and the Arab Spring resolved Europe's long-standing democratisation-stabilisation dilemma in the neighbourhood. This enabled the EU to switch from a policy of containment to a policy of engagement in its relationship with moderate Islamist parties and movements. However, some problems remain. The EU continues to expect Islamist actors to adjust to its own discursive framework by enshrining liberal rights and endorsing established power relations that many Islamists consider hostile. Moreover, while the Arab Spring has temporarily empowered proponents of engagement amongst the EU member states, the perceptions of an impending 'Islamist winter' has cast some doubts over this policy and has stoked intra-European divisions. This will complicate EU attempts to build a new partnership with post-revolutionary Arab democracies and fuel old stereotypes and animosities.

References

Adler, E., ed., *The Convergence of Civilizations: Constructing a Mediterranean Region*. Toronto: University of Toronto Press, 2006.

Ajami, F. *Dream Palace of the Arabs: A Generation's Odyssey*. New York: Pantheon Books, 1998.

Amirah-Fernández, H. and I. Menendez. "Reform in Comparative Perspective: US and EU Strategies of Democracy Promotion in the MENA Region after 9/11". *Journal of Contemporary European Studies* 17, no. 3 (2009): 325–38.

Behr, T. *After the Revolution: The EU and the Arab Transition*, Notre Europe Policy Paper 54. Paris: Notre Europe, 2012.

Behr, T. "The EU and Arab Democracy". In *Hard Choices: The EU's Options in a Changing Middle East*, edited by T. Behr. Helsinki: FIIA, 2011.

Behr, T. *Regional Integration in the Mediterranean: Moving out of the Deadlock?*, Notre Europe Studies & Research 77. Paris: Notre Europe, 2010.

Behr, T. "Enduring Differences? France, Germany and Europe's Middle East Dilemma". *Journal of European Integration* 30, no. 1 (2008): 79–96.

Boubekeur, A. and S. Amghar. *Islamist Parties in the Maghreb and their Links with EU: Mutual Influences and the Dynamics of Democratization*, EuroMeSCo Working Paper 55. Rome: EuroMeSCo, October 2006.

Burgat, F. *Face to Face with Political Islam*. New York: I.B. Tauris, 2005.

Cavatorta, F. and M. Pace. "The Post-normative Turn in European Union (EU)-Middle East and North Africa (MENA) Relations: An Introduction". *European Foreign Affairs Review* 15, no. 5 (2010): 581–7.

Chevènement, J.-P. *Le vert et le noir: intégrisme, pétrole, dollar*. Paris: Grasset, 1995.

Cooper, R. *The Breaking of Nations: Order and Chaos in the Twenty-First Century*. London: Atlantic Books, 2003.

Emerson, M. and R. Youngs. *Political Islam and European Foreign Policy: Perspectives from Muslim Democrats of the Mediterranean*. Brussels: CEPS, 2007.

Entelis, J. P. *Morocco's New Political Face: Plus ça change, plus c'est la même chose*. POMED Policy Brief 5. Washington DC: Project on Middle East Democracy, December 2011.

Esposito, J. L. *The Islamic Threat: Myth or Reality*. New York: Oxford University Press, 1999.

European Commission. "President Prodi participation in the Euro-Mediterranean Parliamentary Forum". MEMO/01/359. Brussels, 8 November 2001.

European Commission. "Remarks of High Representative/Vice-President Catherine Ashton following her meeting with President Morsi". MEMO/12/588. Cairo, 19 July 2012.

European Council. *The EU Strategy for Combating Radicalisation and Recruitment*, 14781/1/05, Brussels, 2005.

European Council. *EU Strategic Partnership with the Mediterranean and the Middle East*. Brussels, June 2004.

Halliday, F. *Islam and the Myth of Confrontation: Religion and Politics in the Middle East*. London: I.B. Tauris, 1996.

Hettne, B. and F. Söderbaum. "Civilian Power or Soft Imperialism?: The EU as a Global Actor and the Role of Interregionalism". *European Foreign Affairs Review* 10, no. 4 (2005): 535–52.

Hurd, E. S. "Political Islam and Foreign Policy in Europe and the United States". *Foreign Policy Analysis* 3, no. 4 (2007): 345–67.

Hyde-Prize, A. *European Security in the Twenty First Century: The Challenge of Multipolarity*. London: Routledge, 2007.

Jofffe, G. "The European Union, Democracy and Counter-Terrorism in the Maghreb". *Journal of Common Market Studies* 46, no. 1 (2008): 147–71.

Johansson-Nogués, E. *Civil Society in Euro-Mediterranean Relations: What Success of EU's Normative Promotion?*, EUI Working Papers 40. Florence: European University Institute, 2006.

Jünemann, A. *Civil Society, its Role and Potential in the Mediterranean Context: Which EU Policies?* EuroMeSCo Brief no. 40. Barcelona: EuroMeSCo, 7 May 2012.

Jünemann, A. "Support for Democracy or Fear of Islamism? Europe and Algeria". In *The Islamic World and the West: An Introduction to Political Cultures and International Relations*, edited by K. Hafez. London: Brill Academic Publishers, 2000.

Kausch, K. "Europe's Engagement with Moderate Islamists". In *Islamist Radicalisation: The Challenge for Euro-Mediterranean Relations*, edited by M. Emerson, K. Kausch and R. Youngs. Madrid: FRIDE, 2009.

Kepel, G. *The War for Muslim Minds: Islam and the West*. Cambridge, MA: Harvard University Press, 2004.

Kienle, E. "Political Reform through Economic Reform? The Southern Mediterranean States Ten Years after Barcelona". In *The Euro-Mediterranean Partnership: Assessing the First Decade*, edited by H. Amirah-Fernández and R. Youngs. Madrid: FRIDE, 2005.

Lewis, B. *What Went Wrong?: The Clash Between Islam and Modernity in the Middle East*. New York: Harper Perennial, 2003.

Manners, I. "Normative Power Europe: A Contradiction in. Terms?". *Journal of Common Market Studies* 40, no. 2 (2002): 235–58.

Ottaway, M. and A. Hamzawy. *Islamists in Politics: The Dynamics of Participation*, Carnegie Papers 98. Washington DC: Carnegie Endowment for International Peace, November 2008.

Pace, M. "The Construction of EU Normative Power". *Journal of Common Market Studies* 45, no. 5 (2007): 1039–62.

Schwedler, J. "Democratization, Inclusion and the Moderation of Islamist Parties". *Development* 50, no. 1 (2007): 56–61.

Seeberg, P. "European Neighbourhood Policy, Post-normativity, and Pragmatism". *European Foreign Affairs Review* 15, no. 5 (2010): 663–79.

Silvestri, S. "Islam and Religion in the EU Political System". *West European Politics* 32, no. 6 (2009): 1212–39.

Spencer, C. "Algeria: France's Disarray and Europe's Conundrum". In *The Middle East and Europe: the Power Deficit*, edited by B. A. Roberson. London: Routledge, 1998.

Tibi, B. "Why They Can't Be Democratic". *Journal of Democracy* 19, no. 3 (2008): 43–8.

Wedeen, L. "Beyond the Crusades: Why Huntington, and Bin Laden, are Wrong". *Middle East Policy* 10, no. 2 (2003): 54–61.

Wickham, C. R. "The Path to Moderation: Strategy and Learning in the Formation of Egypt's Wasat Party". *Comparative Politics* 36, no. 2 (2004): 205–28.

Yacoubian, M. *Engaging Islamists and Promoting Democracy*, USIP Special Report 190. Washington DC: United States Institute of Peace, August 2007.

The French Debate on National Identity and the Sarkozy Presidency: A Retrospective

Jonathan Laurence and Gabriel Goodliffe

Nicolas Sarkozy's presidency presented a mixed record on the issues of Muslim immigration and integration. On the one hand, his administration took novel and constructive steps to advance the integration of Muslim immigrants into French society, notably through the granting of unprecedented official recognition and institutional representation to Islam in the country. On the other, by placing the immigration issue at the centre of his 2012 re-election strategy, he overshadowed and undermined the effectiveness of these integrative policies. Given the country's worsening economic outlook and rising unemployment, immigration is therefore likely to remain as salient and difficult an issue under the new Hollande administration as it was under Sarkozy's.

Although French President Nicolas Sarkozy's term in office did not reveal him to be the across-the-board reformer that his campaign rhetoric suggested he would be, he nonetheless pushed hard on several of French politics' closed doors in an attempt to dismantle *l'exception française* (French exceptionalism) in the era of globalisation – from his efforts to raise the retirement age to returning the country's armed forces to NATO's military command structure. Sarkozy's disruptions of the status quo included his willingness to speak frankly and publicly, in both positive and negative terms, about France's Muslim population and to pursue policies – both affirmative and repressive – in favour of their integration. In a political culture in which the 1905 law separating church and state is held in reverence and secondary affiliations are subordinated to *citoyenneté* (citizenship), Sarkozy's creative use of religion policy as an instrument for integrating immigrants into French society marked a significant departure from his predecessors.[1]

After Sarkozy first gained prominence in national political life in 2002, he consistently asked a set of falsely innocent questions in favour of Muslims' integration, in an environment that was often considered inhospitable to new inquiry. What he will be remembered for most is the question he posed to the entire French nation in the fall of 2009: what does it mean to be French? He posed it by launching a 100-day 'Grand Debate on National Identity' that ended in early 2010. In the course of this debate, 350 town hall meetings were held in France's prefectures and a dedicated website was created that received more than 50,000 contributions. Politicians and civil society actors made speeches, wrote reams of opinion articles, and spoke for hours on televised talk shows. From the outset, the debate was geared towards immigration. The instructions sent to the prefects and most of the comments on the official website centred on immigration and the place of Frenchmen of immigrant origin in the national fabric. The resurgence of concerns over national identity in European countries that are characterised by increasingly ethnically and religiously diverse populations begs the question of the utility of this debate in advancing the integration of immigrants in French society as well as its implications for the country's republican model of citizenship.

This article will argue that the national identity debate was in essence a debate about integration, immigration and Islam. President Sarkozy started the national discussion for contradictory reasons, and there were both merits and drawbacks to how it unfolded. On the one hand, it figured in his long-term overhaul of France's self-understanding as an ethnically diverse and religiously plural nation rather than simply a sea of *citoyens* (citizens). On the other, it also functioned as an electoral appeal to an extreme right-wing electorate that favours a stricter set of boundaries around what it means to be French – including the demand for greater adaptation and integration from those of immigrant origin. In both senses, this debate also marked the end of the French exception in the realm of integration and identity politics.

Why the debate?

The national identity debate that was staged in 2009–10 represented a departure from the manner in which the French president had attempted to break with the recent French past. President Sarkozy always seemed delighted to skate on the thin ice that separated perceptive discourse from demagoguery. Integration Minister Eric Besson stated flatly in autumn 2009 that the debate on national identity would "not focus on immigration and Islam". Yet, given the way the public

---

[1] Laurence, "Sarkozy's Faith in the Republic".

discussion developed, this denial quickly lost credibility. This was partly due to extraneous events that took place around the same time. Four days after the debate was announced, a majority of Swiss voters rejected the construction of minarets on Islamic prayer spaces. The issue of Islam's place in Europe was added to the discussion of the socio-economic challenges to integration when, two weeks into the debate, a French statistical agency released data showing little progress in reducing unemployment in the poorer neighbourhoods where many Muslims live and which had been the sites of prolonged rioting in the fall of 2005. But most importantly, the debate took place in the run-up to the 2010 regional elections in which the far-right *Front National* party again posed a threat to the centre-right government's electoral fortunes. In this sense, President Sarkozy's decision to focus on 'national identity' seemed to his opponents to be cynically aimed at co-opting the residual electoral threat posed by French nativists. As Azouz Begag, a former deputy minister for equal opportunities put it, "This debate shows how pervasive the logic of fishing for Front National voters is becoming in [Sarkozy's] UMP party."[2]

Sarkozy's government was the first to maintain that it is legitimate to talk about identity in the context of France as an immigration society, and that this topic should not remain beyond the pale of democratic politics. Since the early 1980s, the debate on the effects of immigration on French society had been largely abandoned by the principal parties and left to the extreme right. The Front National rose to prominence on a wave of anti-immigrant sentiment – its slogans including "Frenchmen First!" (*Les Français d'abord*) –, tainting the subject of immigration and identity as a legitimate topic of mainstream political discussion. Such a dynamic created an unhealthy situation in which legitimate concerns about the successful integration of French-Maghrebi youth came to be stigmatized as racism and, thus, were not much discussed at all or only in heavily coded terminology evoking the problems of 'the youth', 'the neighbourhoods' (*les quartiers)* and 'safety'. To some extent, these rhetorical practices promoted the growth of the Front National, an anti-establishment movement that excelled in pointing out the dithering of an out-of-touch political elite. Indeed, the party was most successful in the first French elections following the terrorist attacks of 9/11. On 21 April 2002, the party's former leader Jean-Marie Le Pen beat out a dozen other candidates (and profited from the Left's divisions) to make it to the second round of the French presidential election, where he earned the right to face off against the incumbent Jacques Chirac.

Chirac trounced Le Pen by 82.2 percent to 17.9 percent in 2002, but President Sarkozy's decision to open a debate on national identity seven years later marked a less Pyrrhic victory for the far-right agenda. The incorporation of the Front

---

[2] A. Begag, "Sarkozy revient aux themes de la xénophobie et de l'islamophobie", *LeMonde.fr*, 20 January 2010.

National's concerns regarding the 'survival' of French identity into the mainstream provided an outlet for the expression of 'white fears' of immigration. Despite occasional generalisations about minority communities or the expression of plainly racist views, many citizens could see for the first time that their concerns about the future of French society – including on the issues of public safety, social order and the rapidly changing demographic make-up of the country's urban areas — would finally be taken into account.

The other potentially positive aspect of the national debate was that it took a step towards 'asking more' from immigrants and minorities in terms of fitting into mainstream society. While this was somewhat a taboo subject, it fit well within France's demanding 'assimilationist' model of citizenship, compared with the laxer cultural and religious policies of its neighbouring European allies.[3] President Sarkozy thus counted on the approval of most French voters to exert some form of external pressure on immigrant-origin communities to think through their own relation to Frenchness, if only to help these communities weed out the undesirable elements in their midst (such as radical Islamists), prove their *bona fide* citizenship, and affirm their desire to integrate fully with their fellow countrymen.

A negative debate

There were nevertheless several disconcerting aspects to this debate that the French electorate picked up on. As mentioned above, the timing of the national debate made it appear as a blatant attempt to capture the extreme right vote prior to the regional elections in March 2010. In the minds of many pundits, this turned an interesting question and potentially noble exercise into a cynical and overtly partisan enterprise. This also led the discussion to tilt heavily towards immigration and Islam rather than other dimensions that challenge what it means to be French in the 21st century, such as economic globalisation and European unification. One minister said that France must "[e]liminate the cancer of Islamism ... ".[4] Another minister gained notoriety for declaring that she expected young Muslims to stop wearing their baseball hats backwards, to stop using slang, to find a job, to feel French and to love France.[5] But as some social activists argued, it is hard to feel French when such caricatures are casually deployed, when finding a job is almost impossible (non-natives are more than twice as likely to be unemployed as natives[6]) and when daily discrimination is a fact of life.[7]

---

[3] Blatt, "Limits of Immigrant Collective Action, 1968-94".

[4] "Fadela Amara: interdire le burqa pour éradiquer le 'cancer' islamiste", *Agence France Presse,* 15 August 2009.

[5] B. Hugues, "Jeune musulman: les propos controversés de Morano", *Le Figaro*, 16 December 2009.

[6] Gobillon and Selod, "Les déterminants spatiaux du chomage".

[7] "Nadine Morano, elle a un problème avec la jeunesse", *20 Minutes,* 15 December 2009.

Indeed, the debate focused almost exclusively on immigration and Islam, ultimately giving the impression that Islam is incompatible with the republic or, at the very least, that Muslim citizens have to reaffirm their allegiance to the republic before being seen as French, thereby assigning them a separate identity rather than regarding them first and foremost as citizens. This was taken by many to be profoundly anti-republican and anti-*laicité*. For example, Emmanuel Todd accused Sarkozy of promoting "hatred of the other" and suggested that the government was beyond "extreme-right or ultra-right". Todd's assessment of the debate revealed the frustration of class warriors in a post-Marxist age: "The reality is that in every case the ethnic issue is used to make us forget the class issue."[8]

One month into President Sarkozy's Grand Debate, a report was issued on socio-economic conditions in the 'sensitive urban zones' (ZUS) that had gone up in flames during the 2005 riots.[9] The publication of the data cut two ways: it seemed to legitimate the President's sense of urgency about the integration of young Frenchmen of recent immigrant origin, albeit without justifying the underlying focus on identity as the prime variable in socio-economic mobility. However, the data also revealed the ineffectiveness of government policies to date – including Sarkozy's own four years as Interior Minister under President Chirac. There are 751 neighbourhoods classified as ZUS, which are home to 4.4 million inhabitants. The report issued by the National Observatory on Sensitive Urban Zones found that unemployment in the ZUS stood at 16.9 percent (compared to 7.7 percent outside the ZUS); that more than 40 percent of ZUS inhabitants under the age of 24 live below the poverty line (more than twice the rate outside); that 22 percent of ZUS residents had no educational diploma (compared to 10 percent outside); and that 24 percent held a university degree (compared to 38 percent outside). Moreover, the unemployment rate of men between the ages of 15-24 living in the ZUS reached a new high of 41.9 percent at the end of 2008, up from 36.9 percent in 2007. One local mayor in the suburb of Clichy-Sous-Bois outside Paris, where the 2005 rioting began, told *Le Monde* that his area had regressed to a "pre-2005 situation".[10] The government's Deputy Minister for Urban Affairs, Fadéla Amara, responded, "If we had done nothing it would have been much worse."[11] In early December, she said she would try to reduce the number of ZUS in order to concentrate on those in the most dire conditions.[12] But many of Amara's plans for the *banlieues* went unfulfilled. One initiative that aimed to place nearly 50,000 young people in apprenticeships by 2011 resulted in positions for less than

---

[8] E. Todd, "Ce que Sarkozy propose, c'est la haine de l'autre", *Le Monde*, 26 December 2009.
[9] L. Bronner, "Zones urbaines sensibles: des indicateurs dans le rouge", *Le Monde,* 30 November 2009.
[10] L. Bronner, "La logique du ghetto arrange tout le monde", *Le Monde*, 30 November 2009.
[11] L. Bronner, "La politique de la ville sur la sellette", *Le Monde*, 30 November 2009.
[12] *Ibid.*

one-third of applicants by the end of 2009. And of those 12,000 individuals, fewer than 1000 had found actual workplace assignments.

In short, the effect of these dismal statistics on integration, combined with a debate that appeared to focus specifically on immigrants and in particular French Muslims, elicited a negative reaction on the part of those who felt that demands were once again being made of them with no consideration for their own concerns, such as racism, unemployment and Islamophobia. "I am Jean Mohammed of the Bastille!" an op-ed author wrote in *Le Monde*. "I am the heir to liberty, like all children of the French community. I have always been French. And I do not understand why I have been asked about my identity since I was born…. I am the heir to liberty, but not to equality – it seems to me that I will never have that right."[13]

An ironic development

In some ways, it is ironic that the debate on national identity took place under President Sarkozy. After all, as interior minister from May 2002 to March 2004 and again from June 2005 to March 2007, he had fought hard and expended much political capital to make sure that there was a place for Muslims in French institutions – not exactly the message being projected by the national debate. Nonetheless, his midwifery of the *Conseil français du culte musulman* (CFCM) and his gamble to include the leading political Islamic federation in the council revealed his confidence in the country's republican institutions. After becoming president, Sarkozy also personally recruited politicians and advisors of immigrant and Muslim background to serve in his administration – and not only those critical of Islam. In the eight years after he first became involved with state-mosque relations, mosque construction boomed and imam training programs were created by the Interior Ministry.

For these accomplishments of institutional integration alone, the Sarkozy era will be noted by historians for the slow achievement of equality for Islam in the republic.[14] Much of this has occurred through the CFCM, that is, the appointment of national chaplains for the armed forces and the prison system. Islamic representatives are gradually taking their place at the "table of the republic", as former Interior Minister Jean-Pierre Chevènement, who had first conceived of the Council, said at the time.[15] Through his dogged promotion of institutional equality for Muslims in state-religion relations and his insistence upon "positive discrimination" (or "effective equality", as he later rephrased it), Sarkozy provoked

---

[13] M. Aberkane, "Je suis Jean Mohammed de la Bastille!" *Le Monde*, 30 December 2009.
[14] Laurence, "Sarkozy's Faith in the Republic".
[15] Laurence, "From Elysée Salon to Table of the Republic".

indignation for upending the self-conception of the postwar political elite and their understanding of citizenship and *laïcité* in the 21st century.

It could be that the Grand Debate really began when, after winning the presidency in 2007, Sarkozy announced the creation of a new Ministry for Immigration, Integration, National Identity and Co-development. The ministry's title alone contained something for everybody, and plainly intimated the linkages this administration would eventually draw between immigration and identity. It was a signal that immigration and integration issues would no longer be relegated to the euphemistic no-man's land of Social Affairs or Labour Ministries, which pleased immigrants' rights groups. For some observers, however, the formal commitment to something called 'national identity' also seemed to provide evidence of another pact Sarkozy had signed with the pariahs of French politics, the Front National.

Sarkozy co-opted some potentially damaging political opposition from the French left by placing former ideological nemeses in key cabinet positions, from the chief officeholder in the Foreign Ministry (Bernard Kouchner) to Urban Affairs (Fadéla Amara) to Immigration (Eric Besson). His policy mix at the national level attracted many prominent Socialists to join his government. But he also counted on them to look the other way as he pandered to the right-wing swing vote in the regional and local elections that took place during his term, as well as – and perhaps most spectacularly – during the 2012 presidential campaign.

The burqa enters the debate

In June 2009, during President Sarkozy's address to the joint sessions of Parliament, he singled out the Islamic facial veil (he called it the *burqa*, but Anglophones would refer to it as the *niqab*) as being "unwelcome in France".[16] The President ordered a parliamentary commission to study an anti-burqa bill in autumn of 2009. Once again, one could be forgiven for wondering "why now? why this?" and for having the general feeling of *déjà vu* following the 2004 headscarf ban in primary and secondary schools, a ban that Sarkozy initially opposed and then reluctantly supported.[17] Journalistic descriptions of the "sudden increase" in burqas could have just had the date changed from 2004 to 2009 and the word "headscarf" replaced with "burqa". Even the number of "perpetrators" (or "victims", depending on one's perspective) was estimated by experts to be virtually the same: out of a potential face-covering population of more than two million, around 1900 women in France were estimated to be burqa-wearers, the same number as the girls who wore a headscarf to school. Of these 1900 women, 270

---

[16] "Sarkozy: La burqa n'est pas la bienvenue sur le territoire de la République", *Libération*, 22 June 2009.
[17] Laurence and Vaisse, *Integrating Islam*.

lived in French overseas territories/departments (e.g. Mayotte and Réunion).[18] In this regard, the burqa issue appeared to be nothing more than low-hanging political fruit, an easy way for the president to attract news coverage and seize momentum during a lull in his presidency.

Whereas there had been genuine debate in France in 2003–04 over whether headscarves constituted a 'religious prescription', there was general consensus in 2009–10 that facial coverings were not a required Islamic practice. A more generous way to put this would be that it was perhaps Sarkozy's confidence that the burqa was such a minor issue affecting so few women that led him to assume that he could limit the fallout by continuing to respect the practice of 'everyday' Islam: namely, by making sure that those Muslims who chose to practice their religion could do so with dignity.

Sarkozy is a rare breed of politician who was willing to say what he thought to French Muslims himself rather than delegate state-mosque relations to his advisors as his predecessors had done. When he was in charge of religion policy at the Interior Ministry, he was the first to show up at community meetings and negotiate personally with religious leaders. The secretary general of an Islamist group outside of Paris once said in an interview that none of the young people he knew would ever deign to vote for Sarkozy. But when he finished that sentence, he added that he, personally, would not vote for anyone else.[19] For many mosque leaders, at least, Sarkozy's efforts were not forgotten. The head of the CFCM, Mohamed Moussaoui, announced, "We will not ask French society to accept the burqa." Many French Muslims, however, felt that their community was being unfairly stigmatized by renewed attention to their religion's garb.[20]

Since well before the riots of 2005, Sarkozy unashamedly appealed to what in American electoral terms would be known as the 'security moms' of French society who want more law and order and less delinquency. But it must be recalled that this target audience also included many residents of the very *banlieues* that he targeted. As was the case with the broader debate on national identity, many considered the French government's ban on the burqa suspect due to its timing just prior to the regional elections. Furthermore, Sarkozy's attempt to monopolise the national identity debate had begun to grate on the nerves of those who might otherwise have agreed with his emphasis on the burqa, including many prominent supporters of *laïcité* who might have been expected to embrace the 'republican' nature of the government's attempt to ban it. But his presentation of the burqa as a pressing social issue was viewed as peculiar and unhelpful to integration. The historian Patrick Weil, a fervent supporter of the headscarf ban in French public schools,

---

[18] C. Gabizon, "Deux mille femmes portent la burqa en France", *Le Figaro*, 8 September 2009.

[19] Interview conducted by J. Laurence and J. Vaisse in March 2007.

[20] F. Khosrokhavar, "Burqa: une loi pourrait renforcer les extrèmes du fondamentalisme", *Le Monde*, 21 October 2009.

who sat on the commission that proposed it, wrote that a burqa ban could never be enforced in "the street…, a common public space where one enjoys the most individual liberties". He added, however, that "it is possible to conceive of internal rules in companies or in public places that could require one's face to be visible".[21]

One year after President Sarkozy's speech declaring the burqa "unwelcome", in July 2010 the National Assembly approved a bill that would impose a fine of several hundred euros on anyone covering their face in public and imprisonment for anyone forcing someone else to do so. Soon thereafter, a wealthy French Muslim announced a fund to reimburse any woman who received a fine. Just as the veil law in French schools passed relatively unnoticed in 2004,[22] so too did the infamous burqa bill pass without much fanfare. It helped that the Sheikh of Al-Azhar – for many Sunni Muslims the closest thing to a centre of religious authority – reiterated the institution's opposition to facial veils, and that the governments of Syria and Egypt soon followed suit with their own burqa bans on university campuses, indicating that they share some of the same concerns as the French government.[23]

The end of the French exception

The debate on national identity that took place in France during Sarkozy's presidency, when combined with his recognition of an official instance of representation for the French Muslim community in the form of the CFCM, signalled the end of an era, namely that of a stubborn refusal to re-open the debate on the French integration model, and of the country's confidence in the republican institutions on which the model depended. Indeed, if one examines the record of President Sarkozy and his lieutenants over a ten-year period, he is the single person who did the most for French Muslims in their quest for institutional equality – from mosque building to imam training, from political appointments to university admissions.

In the 1990s, when Germans were considering whether or not to grant citizenship to Turkish nationals born on German soil, they pointed to France as a prime example of the disconnect between nationality and allegiance under a model of citizenship based on *ius soli* (though now, with the children of immigrants having to choose between the French and their parents' nationalities, an element of *ius sanguinis* has been mixed in).[24] Resurrecting a term used by their countrymen over a century earlier, German newspapers spoke disdainfully of the *Français de papier*

---

[21] Fontaine, "La burqa est bannie de l'espace politique"; see also Weil, *Liberté, égalité, discriminations*.
[22] Laurence and Vaisse, *Integrating Islam*.
[23] S. Abdoun, "Minister says no Niqab in Universities this Year", *The Daily News* (Egypt), 27 July 2010.
[24] Brubaker, *Citizenship and Nationhood in France and Germany*.

who were not first asked to demonstrate a commitment to acquiring French nationality, as Germany's *ius sanguinis*-based citizenship law required at the time. This foreshadowed the debates of the decade that followed in nearly every European country featuring significant immigrant minorities.[25] What should be required of such so-called 'newcomers'? Throughout the seventies and eighties, French politicians were so convinced of the capacity of republican institutions to integrate immigrants that they got away with speaking about *jeunes* and *quartiers* instead of calling certain categories by their real names.[26]

In this limited sense, the changes wrought by ten years of 'life with Sarkozy' marked a healthy development. He had the political instinct to take account of growing demands for recognition and institutional equality among Muslim communities. He also had the courage to talk about building mosques – a process which, though begun under previous governments, had never been as publicised – and to raise the possibility of affirmative action, whereas his predecessors were content to build more recreation rooms in the *banlieues* and to funnel money into a vaguely defined *politique de la ville* that largely ignored the cultural and religious dimensions of integration, choosing to view it instead as an exclusively socio-economic problem.[27]

Even though it may have been introduced for cynical political motives, what the advent of the debate on national identity signified, then, was perhaps the end of the French exception. To ask "what does it mean to be French?" in 2010 was to acknowledge that slogans about *liberté, égalité* and *fraternité* no longer sufficed as an answer, and to admit that the French were as susceptible to self-doubt regarding their identity as the post-Imperial British or the postwar Germans. Or to put the question in different terms, to ask what it means to be French is to acknowledge a loss of control over not just a growing Muslim population, but also the rising tide of Islamophobia or growing ambivalence about the Muslim presence. It is a belated recognition of the grassroots frustration felt by many voters – whether political elites like it or not – confronted with the increased visibility of non-European immigrants within French society.

The French Immigration Ministry reported that many French citizens hold very similar criteria with regard to integrating immigrants as their European neighbours. According to the thousands who logged onto the official website of the national identity debate website in 2009–10, "being French" means, in order of popularity:

1. shared beliefs and values
2. shared nationality
3. shared religion or a shared relationship to religion

---

[25] Leveau *et al.*, *New European Identity and Citizenship*.
[26] Laurence, "Sarkozy's Faith in the Republic".
[27] *Ibid.*

4. family origins
5. French language
6. geographic origins.[28]

By the same token, this debate also reflected the specifically French circumstances in which it was being conducted. The discussion of the burqa ban occurred in the context of the ongoing and fraught discussion of what constitutes the public sphere and of what is acceptable behaviour within it. It re-opened discussion of the mythical dictums that defined 19th century religious politics: "being a Jew at home and a citizen in the street", or "denying the Jews as a nation everything and granting them everything as individuals". Thus, it marked the evolution of the French secular concept of *laïcité* from guaranteeing a neutral public space to meddling with the practices of those who use that space.

Post-script to the national debate: the 2012 presidential election

Regrettably, the advances registered by Sarkozy in terms of acknowledging and moving to rectify the lack of institutional organisation and representation afforded immigrants and, in particular, Muslims, in France were offset by his polarising attempts to use the immigration issue as a means to maximise his electoral clout and, specifically, in a replay of 2007, to wean votes from the Front National. These efforts came to a head in the 2012 presidential campaign, and did much to undo the gains and dispel the goodwill achieved among immigrants and their organisational representatives during the early years of his term. Thus, in the attempt to outdo Front National leader Marine Le Pen in the "tough on immigration" stakes, Sarkozy successively pledged to make naturalisation harder for immigrants born of non-French parents and to forbid naturalisation of immigrants found guilty of certain categories of crimes, followed Marine Le Pen in calling for the labeling of 'halal' meat, threatened to pull France out of the Schengen customs union unless its other members clamped down on illegal immigration, and arrested and expelled Muslim fundamentalists across the country (this particularly in the wake of the shooting spree in Toulouse and Montauban on the part of a French al-Qaeda sympizer of Algerian descent).[29] In turn, these rather transparent attempts to

---

[28] "Grand Débat sur l'identité nationale. Pour vous, c'est quoi être français? Analyse des contributions", *TNS Sofres,* 4 January 2010, http://www.debatidentitenationale.fr/participation/pour-vous-quest-ce-qu-etre/.

[29] P. Weil "Les quatres piliers de la nationalité", *Le Monde.fr*, 23 August 2010, http://www.lemonde.fr/idees/article/2010/08/23/les-quatre-piliers-de-la-nationalite-par-patrick-weil_1401781_3232.html; H. Alexander, "France election 2012: Islam takes centre stage in battle for France," *Daily Telegraph* (online), 8 April 2012, http://www.telegraph.co.uk/news/worldnews/europe/france/9191923/France-election-2012-Islam-takes-centre-stage-in-battle-for-France.html; A. Chrisafis, "Nicolas Sarkozy Courts Rightwing Voters with Schengen Zone Threat", *Guardian* (online), 11 March 2012, http://www.guardian.co.uk/world/2012/mar/11/nicolas-sarkozy-french-elections-2012.

co-opt the FN's electorate culminated in Sarkozy's assertions, between the first and second rounds of voting, that Marine Le Pen is "compatible with the republic" and that the FN is "a democratic party" like any other.[30]

In successive rounds of voting in the 2010 regional elections, 2011 local elections and 2012 presidential and parliamentary elections, voters pronounced themselves on the effectiveness of this strategy. It is plain to see that Sarkozy's efforts to exploit the immigration issue for political gain failed to minimise the electoral damage he faced as an incumbent in the context of a tanking economy and disappearing jobs, as well as to contain the further expansion of the Front National. Thus, after his party suffered substantial setbacks in the 2010 regional and 2011 local elections, Sarkozy was himself defeated by the Socialist Party (PS) candidate François Hollande by 51.6 percent to 48.4 percent in the second round of the 2012 presidential election, but not before Marine Le Pen obtained 17.9 percent of the vote in the first round, thereby breaking the record score by which her father acceded to the second round run-off in 2002. Meanwhile, his Union for a Popular Movement (UMP) party lost its majority in the National Assembly, with the PS winning 40.9 percent of the vote versus 37.9 percent for the UMP in the second round, giving the former and its allies 295 out of 577 deputies, versus 196 for the latter.[31]

At one level, these results, particularly the Front National's strong scores in the first round of the presidential and parliamentary elections (where it received 13.6 percent of the vote nationally), suggest that Sarkozy's attempt to instrumentalise the immigration issue for political gain backfired as it coincided with the electoral resurgence of the extreme right. More broadly, the record level of abstention that characterised the first round of the parliamentary election (42.8 percent vs. 39.6 percent in 2007) testified to a growing disengagement on the part of French voters from the electoral process.[32] In short, Sarkozy's cynical use of national identity as a wedge issue ended up fuelling mistrust of the political class and a belief that politicians are unable to solve the genuine problems faced by contemporary societies.

Conclusion

Many Muslims living in France and other European countries have felt stigmatized by their religious background and experience the sensation that the walls are closing in on them. A flurry of restrictive legislation marked the first decade of this century: governments in France and Germany passed laws to prohibit mainstream

---

[30] D. Bell, "Midnight in Paris", *The New Republic* (online), 4 May 2012, http://www.tnr.com/article/world/magazine/103093/nicolas-sarkozy-marine-le-pen-ump-france-election.

[31] Ministère de l'intérieur, "Les résultats des élections législatives 2012", http://www.interieur.gouv.fr/sections/a_votre_service/resultats-elections/LG2012/.

[32] P. Perrineau, "Quelle majorité pour la gauche à l'Assemblée nationale?" *Le Figaro*, 12 June 2012.

religious symbols such as minarets and headscarves, as well as less widespread cultural practices associated with the Islamic world like burqas, polygamy and forced marriages. Official and informal opposition to mosque construction is increasingly commonplace, as is the conditioning of naturalisation on 'moderate' religious practice.

On the one hand, it could be argued that such opposition will continue to be fanned by the initiatives that were taken by the Sarkozy government, such as the debate on national identity, the ban on the burqa, and the implicitly anti-immigrant tenor of his 2012 presidential campaign. While emboldening the most xenophobic elements of the 'native' French population, these initiatives could also drive immigrant and minority communities inward and lead to their feeling *less* French as a result. In this respect, however, they overlook the larger picture of integration – namely, the fact that daily integration *is* taking place. By focusing on a handful of specific problems, French voters have been led to mistake the tree for the forest. Social and economic issues have been largely ignored, as have the challenges of racism and Islamophobia. But this has been addressed in other, less sensational fora, especially during the institutionalisation of state-mosque relations and the creation of the CFCM.

The negative rhetoric and repressive measures that have put Muslim communities on the defensive belie the broader trend towards greater official recognition and institutional representation for Islam initiated under Sarkozy, even in the context of toughening rhetoric on national identity. The gestures of restriction and toleration are in fact complementary and part of the same process. French and European Muslims are in the throes of a distilled and abbreviated era of emancipation: a dual movement of expanding religious liberty *and* increasing control over religion. By restricting visible Islamic symbols, host societies are tracing the outer limits of practices they consider beyond the pale. But there is much more *within the pale* that is now treated as routine, including the institutionalisation of state-mosque relations in representative bodies like the CFCM. European governments have implemented new policies raising standards and expectations for the integration of newcomers, with increasing restrictions on citizenship being accompanied by greater equality before the law.

More ominously, however, no clear path or progression seems available for addressing the deepening economic and social inequalities that, due to the accelerating dynamics and intensifying impacts of globalisation, are giving ever greater salience to ethnic and religious divisions within the country. In this respect, the Socialist government, although it appears to be more solicitous and tolerant of immigrants,[33] is unlikely to be able to attenuate the social fallout

---

[33] "Manuel Valls va revenir sur certains critères de la naturalisation", *Le Monde*.fr (online), 25 July 2012, http://www.lemonde.fr/politique/article/2012/07/25/manuel-valls-va-revenir-sur-certains-criteres-de-naturalisation_1738291_823448.html.

from globalisation. This is sure to keep the problems linked to immigration on the front pages and to make them as salient an issue under Hollande as they were under Sarkozy.

References

Blatt, D. "Towards a Multi-cultural Political Model in France? The Limits of Immigrant Collective Action, 1968–94". *Nationalism and Ethnic Politics* 1, no. 2 (2005): 156–77.

Brubaker, R. *Citizenship and Nationhood in France and Germany.* Cambridge, MA: Harvard University Press, 1992.

Fontaine, C. "Patrick Weil: La burqa est bannie de l'espace politique, pas de la rue". *Paris Match,* 2 July 2009.

Gobillon, L. and H. Selod. "Les déterminants spatiaux du chomage". In *Ségrégation urbaine, intégration sociale*, edited by J.P. Fitoussi, E. Laurent, and J. Maurice: 171–87. Paris: Conseil d'analyse économique, 2003.

Laurence, J. "From an Elysée Salon to the Table of the Republic". *French Politics, Culture and Society* 23, no. 1 (2005): 37–65.

Laurence, J. and J. Vaisse. *Integrating Islam: Political and Religious Challenges in Contemporary France.* Washington, DC: Brookings Press, 2006.

Laurence, J. "Sarkozy's Faith in the Republic". *The Tocqueville Review/La Revue Tocqueville* XXX, no. 1 (2009): 159–81.

Leveau, R., K. Mohsen-Finan and C. Wihtol de Wenden, eds. *New European Identity and Citizenship.* Burlington, VT: Ashgate, 2002.

Weil, P. *Liberté, égalité, discriminations. L'identité nationale au regard de l'histoire.* Paris: Grasset, coll. Folio, 2009.

Muslim Organisations and Intergenerational Change in Germany

Dirk Halm

The process of social integration of the people associated with immigrant organisations, and the social (and potentially religious) change that comes with it, present the organisations with the difficult challenge of justifying their legitimacy to various societal actors. This is certainly true of Muslim organisations in Western immigration societies. In Germany, this process is quite clearly reflected within the community of established organisations, which play a part in creating intergenerational change. This is not to say, however, that they will be the only relevant – or even the predominant – actors involved in establishing Islam in Germany in the future, despite their roots in their countries of origin, nor that they will automatically become redundant over time.

Recognition of the need for long-term integration of different groups into German society has been slow to take root. The first attempt at a systematic approach to integration policy on the federal level coincided with a shift in the integration debate: Germany began to discuss immigrant integration issues at a time when security, Islam and cultural difference took on great importance mainly as a result of 9/11 and the ensuing events. As a result, the integration and the security discourse intermingled, even though Islam was still far from being considered an established religion in Germany, lacking as it does the kind of structures that correspond to the specific German framework of religious policy.

Many of these problems have been addressed by the German Islam Conference of representatives of both the state and the Muslim community, which has been taking place since 2006. Yet, the community of Islamic organisations has faced enormous challenges in the last decade.[1] Not only have these organisations found themselves confronted with an increasingly suspicious German society, especially in

---

[1] Halm, "The Current Discourse on Islam in Germany".

the context of the public debates on terrorism – a situation that has forced them to position themselves clearly – they have also had to promote the socio-political and institutional integration of a major religious community with some four million believers[2] and to justify their legitimacy both to their members and to German society. This is all the more difficult because the question of which organisations should be regarded as legitimate representatives of the Muslims has itself been a major focus of the debate. As a result, the importance of the larger, often Turkish-dominated associations has been put into perspective rather than reconfirmed.

There have been relatively few empirically grounded studies of this issue. In fact, the only representative study in this area indicates that only a minority of Muslims consider themselves represented by the large associations which established the Coordination Council of Muslims in Germany (KRM) during the German Islam Conference.[3]

Regardless of how important individual Muslim organisations are at the moment, the expectations the actors involved have of these organisations will change as the new generations grow up, and so will the community within which the organisations have to justify their legitimacy. The inability to cope with these various challenges may contribute to the decline in power of established Muslim organisations. As regards Muslim policy in Germany, such a development would be consistent with a widespread discourse which considers the established organisations and associations to be of little (and, most importantly, of diminishing) relevance.

This article examines the consequences for Muslim organisations of intergenerational change in the Muslim community in Germany by asking to what extent this change takes place inside or outside the established organisational structures. This question is important when trying to estimate the future role of the organisations in Muslim claims making. Should the impact of the established organisations shrink in the long run, one would have to ask how an alternative representation of Muslim interests could be shaped. The survey on which the article is based, sponsored by the European Integration Fund (EIF) and the German Federal Office for Migration and Refugees (BAMF) on behalf of the German Islam Conference,[4] was carried out in 2011.

Before presenting these results, the following sections provide a brief discussion of intergenerational change and some basic information about organised Islam in Germany.

---

[2] The Federal Office for Migration and Refugees (BAMF) estimates the Muslim population in Germany to be between 3.8 and 4.3 million, with 2.5 to 2.7 million of the Muslims resident in Germany being of Turkish ancestry (Haug *et al.*, *Muslimisches Leben in Deutschland*, 80–3).

[3] *Ibid.*, 179. However, it should also be noted that the perceived size of an association's membership is always determined by the way questions (on membership, sympathies, feeling of being represented, etc.) are worded.

[4] See also Halm and Sauer, "Islamische Gemeinden in Deutschland".

Intergenerational change in Muslim religiousness

Recent studies on intergenerational change in Muslim religiousness in Germany indicate that attitudes are becoming increasingly disparate and that individualisation and a strong sense of religiousness are not necessarily mutually exclusive.[5] Indeed, religious orientation is taking on growing importance among second and later generations of migrants, which may also be interpreted as a result of the specific conditions of social integration in Germany.

In a study on the religiousness of German Muslims complementary to the worldwide, religious studies-oriented representative Bertelsmann Religion Monitor carried out in 2008,[6] qualitative interviews with Sunni German Muslims revealed a pattern which is of great relevance for the present article. Of the three categories of believers established in the study, one is of interviewees born in Germany who associate their religiousness with a search for meaning. They do not attend the traditional mosques and their origins as immigrants do not play a major role in the way they construct their identities as Muslims. Nevertheless, religiousness in this group is above average and manifests itself in a wide range between orthodox practice and individualised personal faith.[7]

It is safe to assume, then, that organised Islam in Germany will indeed face significant religious change and increasing disparity in parts of the Muslim community in Germany and that certain characteristics of the traditional organisations may not be compatible with the new requirements.

Corresponding with the Muslim population structure in Germany, the Muslim organisational field is dominated by mosques especially connected with Turkey. Those mosques originally organised believers from the 'guest workers' migration, strongly oriented towards their countries of origin, preponderantly Turkey. This background manifests itself in the organisations' use of the (Turkish) language . Yet, due to intergenerational change, cultural and religious identities may come to the forefront, diminishing the significance of national ancestry and strengthening the mere immigrant background instead.[8] Accordingly, with regard to the self-organisation of migrants in Germany in general, Dietrich Thränhardt has stated that:

> Groups made up of people from different origins have the special advantage of incorporating diversity within themselves and thus have an inherently integrative effect. [...] They are better suited to meet the needs of the "second" and "third" generations who grow up in Germany.[9]

---

[5] See Klinkhammer, *Moderne Formen islamischer Lebensführung*; Tietze, *Islamische Identitäten*; Boos-Nünning and Karakaşoğlu, *Viele Welten leben*.

[6] Thielmann, "Vielfältige muslimische Religiosität in Deutschland". An additional two thousand German Muslims were interviewed for this survey.

[7] Halm, "The Current Discourse on Islam in Germany".

[8] Tietze, *Islamische Identitäten*, 237.

[9] Thränhardt, *Selbstorganisationen von Migrantinnen und Migranten*, 3.

In addressing the question of whether and how organisations will meet the changing needs of their members or potential users, considerations of organisational sociology come into focus. One significant aspect in this regard is the fact that an organisation's ability to adapt to the needs of its members is affected by a wide variety of conditions. There are many competing interests in any organisation, and the need to justify one's activities to actors outside the organisation can lead to conflicts with the members' expectations. In some cases, mosque communities and their associations must justify their activities not only to their members and users, but also to other social actors and institutions from the country of origin, the receiving country or elsewhere.

Organised Islam in Germany

The BAMF survey results show that only roughly one quarter of Muslims felt represented by the Coordination Council of Muslims comprising the Islamic Council, DITIB (*Türkisch-Islamische Union der Anstalt für Religion* – Turkish-Islamic Union for Religious Affairs), ZMD (*Zentralrat der Muslime in Deutschland* – Central Council of Muslims in Germany) and VIKZ (*Verband der Islamischen Kulturzentren* – Association of Islamic Cultural Centres).[10] However, 86 percent of respondents in the BAMF study described themselves as somewhat or very 'religious'. The BAMF study emphasizes the disconnect between the strong religiousness, on the one hand, and the low degree of organisation, on the other. Accordingly, in the Bertelsmann survey it emerged that only 42 percent of respondents categorised as highly religious (41 percent of the sample) regularly attended a mosque.[11]

In terms of reach, the following four associations are the most important in Germany today:

- The DITIB, founded on the initiative of the Presidency of Religious Affairs to establish mosques that conform to the concept of *laïcité*.
- The IGMG (*Islamische Gemeinschaft Milli Görüs* – Milli Görüs Islamic Association), the largest non-state-affiliated Sunni organisation.
- The VIKZ, representing a mystic Sunni brand of Islam.
- The AABF (*Alevitische Gemeinde Deutschland* – Alevi Community Germany), the most important Alevi association in Germany.[12]

---

[10] Haug *et al.*, *Muslimisches Leben in Deutschland*, 179.

[11] Thielmann, "Vielfältige muslimische Religiosität in Deutschland", 6–7.

[12] In recent years, the question of whether or not the Alevi should be considered members of the Islamic community has been widely debated, especially among the Alevi themselves. The special situation in Germany is that the AABF may have emphasised the independence of Alevism for tactical political reasons to achieve recognition both as a religious community and as an independent point of contact for political actors, even though this image may not necessarily be consistent with the image the individual believers have of this group (for a detailed discussion of these developments, see Sökefeld, "Difficult Identifications"; Halm *et. al.*, "Polish and Turkish Migrant Organizations", 64).

The Sunni 'umbrella organisations', the Central Council of Muslims in Germany (ZMD) and the Islamic Council, of which IGMG is a member, do not include VIKZ and DITIB. As already mentioned, the German Islam Conference also led to the creation of the Coordination Council of Muslims in Germany (KRM), comprising the DITIB, ZMD, Islamic Council and VIKZ.

Recent case studies on the large Muslim associations in Germany reveal considerable dynamics.[13] They respond to a rather high degree to the needs and demands of different and changing users. Against this background, Rosenow sees German integration policy and the activities of the DITIB association merging, resulting in increasing use of the German language in mosques, the differentiation of organisational structures to fit in the German federal system, more professional management and more activities related to social integration.[14] Nevertheless, DITIB still has to balance loyalties to Germany and Turkey, which is no easy task despite all the re-orientation in recent years.

In contrast to DITIB, which to a considerable extent relies on the Turkish state (which educates and employs the DITIB imams), relations between Milli Görüs and Turkey have undergone substantial changes in the last decades. Milli Görüs was closely related to the Islamist Erbakan movement in Turkey, which was weakened considerably by the ban on its political branches in the 1990s. As a consequence, the opportunity structure and the transnational organisational field shifted, resulting in a re-orientation toward the Muslim diaspora in Europe and the pragmatic needs of Muslim immigrants, which had to be weighed against Islamist ideas and values.[15] Today, Milli Görüs combines the strengthening of Muslim identities with unflinching engagement for better education and social integration of its users.

The cited research shows that, generally speaking, the Muslim associations in Germany have a great potential to adapt to the changing conditions. However, whether or not they will be able to activate this potential depends on a variety of factors. At the same time, the case studies make clear that the generational change does indeed present a major challenge for the organisations.

Intergenerational change in Muslim organisations

The data on intergenerational change in Muslim organisations in Germany derives from a telephone (and, in a few cases, postal) survey of 1,141 Muslim, including Alevi, religious organisations in 2011.[16]

---

[13] Rosenow, "Von der Konsolidierung zur Erneuerung"; Schiffauer, *Parallelgesellschaften*.

[14] Rosenow, *Ibid.*

[15] Schiffauer, *Parallelgesellschaften*; Halm *et al.*, "Polish and Turkish Migrant Organizations".

[16] They were chosen out of the 2,342 organisations with prayer rooms whose contact information proved to be valid in the course of the survey. The sample was not representative, as it was not randomly chosen and the main unit of all mosques in Germany it applies to is to a certain extent unknown, although an extensive list of organisations based on multiple research strategies (interviews with local authorities,

Insight into social and intergenerational change within the organisations can be gained by observing the immigrant background of the organisation's operatives and visitors, but also the language spoken during religious services and the degree to which believers from different origins are involved.

Table 1. Immigrant background of chairman and of predominant visitors (% of all organisations interviewed)

	Chairman	Predominant visitors
1st generation	21.9	14.7
2nd generation or younger	59.2	45.9
Marriage migration	9.7	1.0
Refugees/asylum	0.8	0.4
No immigrant background	3.9	1.1
Other	1.0	0.3
No predominant group	–	33.3
Don't know	1.8	1.3
No reply	1.7	2.1
Total	100	100

About half of the organisations today are dominated by successors of the first immigrant generation or are run by such operatives. Another third are not dominated by any immigrant generation. Generally, one cannot assume that a majority of a certain background in an organisation means that they thoroughly bestride the community. On the contrary, visitors from all groups can be found in most of the organisations, with the exception of refugees and believers without an immigrant background. But even the latter were present in 43 percent of the organisations in which interviews were carried out.

As a consequence, the organisations normally have no clear first or second generation immigrant profile. This finding is strengthened by observing the statistical correlation between the immigrant backgrounds of chairmen and visitors. There is a positive correlation, in that in organisations with second generation chairmen, second generation visitors tend to predominate, but the correlation is weak (Cramers V: 0.180; significance: <0.01).[17]

(*footnote continued*)
gathering of scientific data, interviews with Muslim associations, online research) existed. Nevertheless, a comparison of the (revised) contact list with the interviews carried out with regard to the available attributes of adherence to a certain Muslim branch (Sunni, Alevi etc.) and membership in associations shows that the interviews fairly represent the contact list regarding those attributes. The share of DITIB organisations for instance is 48 percent in the revised contact list and 45 percent in the interviews.

[17] This argument may be challenged by the reasoning that the correlation must be relatively weak for technical considerations, as chairpersons may well come from smaller groups like marriage migrants, but these groups will hardly be predominant among a mosque's visitors.

Table 2. Predominant visitors with respect to immigrant background of chairmen (% of all organisations)*

	Immigrant background of chairman			
	1st generation	2nd generation or younger	Marriage migration	No predominant group
Predominant visitors				
1st generation	41.6	43.4	8.4	4.2
2nd generation or younger	17.8	69.4	9.3	2.2
Marriage migration	9.1	45.5	45.5	–
No predominant group	22.2	60.4	10.7	4.8
Total	22.7	61.5	10.2	3.8

*without "don't know" and "no reply". Missing percent: refugees/asylum, other.

At the same time, the correlation between the length of time an organisation has existed and the immigrant background of the predominant visitors (Cramers V: 0.099; significance <0.05) and the chairman (Cramers V: 0.1; significance <0.01) is also weak.

Table 3. Immigrant background of chairman and predominant visitors in relation to the length of time the organisation exists (% of all organisations)

	Year of foundation				
	Before 1970	1970–79	1980–89	1990–99	Since 2000
Immigrant background of chairman					
1st generation	2.1	15.6	35.9	32.1	14.3
2nd generation or younger	1.4	20.9	36.2	30.3	11.1
Marriage migration	0.9	13.2	35.8	35.8	14.2
No immigrant background	7.5	7.5	35.0	22.5	27.5
Predominant visitors					
1st generation	1.2	20.5	39.1	27.3	11.8
2nd generation or younger	0.8	20.8	32.9	32.9	12.7
No predominant group	3.6	14.9	39.2	29.3	13.0

Membership in a mosque association is significantly linked to the immigrant background of the chairman. This is especially true with regard to the DITIB (Cramers V: 0.160; significance <0.001), 'free' organisations (Cramers V: 0.158; significance <0.001) and mosques that are affiliated to more than one association (Cramers V: 0.136; significance <0.01). Observing the link between membership and predominant visitor groups, there are significant correlations for DITIB (Cramers V: 0.139; significance <0.01) and IGMG (Cramers V: 0.171; significance <0.001) members. Especially the larger associations, DITIB, IGMG and

VIKZ, are run by second generation chairmen and visited by the second generation more often than average (in over 50 percent of the cases). They represent the guest worker immigration of the 1960s and 1970s and families with a rather long duration of stay in Germany, having raised children and grandchildren there.

The AABF, the smaller associations and the 'free' organisations, instead, display above average shares of first generation visitors, even though the majority of chairmen come from the second generation. While the findings indicate that 'free' communities and smaller associations tend to draw immigrant groups with a shorter overall presence in Germany, the explanation for the relatively high share of first generation visitors in AABF *cem* houses is not clear.

Table 4. Immigrant background of chairman and predominant visitors with respect to membership in associations (% of all organisations)

	Membership						
	DITIB	IGMG	VIKZ	AABF	Other	'Free'	Total
Immigrant background of chairman							
1st generation	17.9	15.7	16.2	25.0	30.4	32.3	22.7
2nd generation or younger	66.1	69.0	72.4	60.0	53.4	51.3	61.3
Marriage migration	11.8	11.1	8.6	15.0	6.8	8.0	10.1
No immigrant background	2.8	3.7	2.2	–	6.8	5.3	4.1
Cramers V	0.160***	0.103*	0.101*	–	0.136**	0.158***	–
Predominant visitors							
1st generation	15.9	14.8	15.1	25.6	16.7	15.8	15.2
2nd generation or younger	52.9	62.5	56.2	38.5	42.0	46.9	47.5
No predominant group	28.0	19.9	28.1	30.8	36.7	35.4	34.5
Cramers V	0.139**	0.171***	–	–	–	–	–

Levels of significance: ***<0.001, **<0.01, *<0.05, – = not significant

Intergenerational change thus takes place within the large, established, Turkish dominated, Sunni organisations and associations, rather than by replacing established mosques with younger ones that may have weaker national identities. This probably has to do with the ability of the aforementioned, established mosques to integrate groups with varying backgrounds and origins. In two out of three organisations, visitors come from more than one country of origin. 43 percent of the interviewees mention three or more countries of origin (two origins: 25 percent). But at the same time, in 64 percent of the organisations, over 70 percent of believers are of Turkish origin.

Regarding the language of religious services, (multiple answers permitted), the languages of the countries of origin clearly dominate (85 percent of services), but a considerable minority (37 percent) uses the German language and 25 percent offer a German translation. As expected, the use of German language correlates with the heterogeneity of the visitors attending the services. In strongly Turkish dominated mosques, the use of German is less frequent than in the others.

Table 5. Predominant origin of visitors with respect to the language of religious services (% of all organisations, multiple answers allowed)

	German	Language of origin	Arab	German translation	Translation into language of origin	Other
Predominant group						
Turks	31.5	96.6	22.8	27.9	2.2	3.8
None	66.1	28.6	66.1	21.4	3.6	17.9

Conclusion

Muslim organisations in Germany are faced with the divergent tasks of increasing their organisational muscle while at the same time allowing more heterogeneity and reform.

Overall, representation of Islam in Germany through organisations is rather weak and there are indications that the organisations' ability to incorporate believers is not increasing, especially since believers born in Germany display more and more individualised concepts of Muslim religiousness. Yet, though the large Turkish associations are far from being representative of the Muslim community in Germany, there are no viable alternatives on the horizon that can challenge their role in providing basic religious infrastructure and services (provision of imams, prayer, pilgrimages, funerals, weddings, etc.).

In practice, the problem of specific countries of origin – namely Turkey – and therefore languages of origin dominating the mosques seems to be of minor importance, since attendance by believers from more than one country is the general rule and, even in the largely Turkey-oriented mosques, use of the German language is slowly increasing.

Heterogeneity and intergenerational change is manifest *inside* the reality of Islamic organisations today. That said, it must be conceded that traditional Islam, as represented by the established organisations, mostly connected to Turkey, do play more than a minor role for Muslims in Germany. That notwithstanding, the march of intergenerational change in the Muslim community may chip away at the importance of the traditional organisations in the long run. Nevertheless, this may not lead automatically to an erosion of the current Muslim organisations or the establishment of alternative organisations on a large scale, as the organisations themselves may be able to cope with social change.

References

Boos-Nünning, U. and Y. Karakaşoğlu. *Viele Welten leben: Zur Lebenssituation von Mädchen und jungen Frauen mit Migrationshintergrund*. Münster: Waxmann, 2005.

Halm, D. "The Current Discourse on Islam in Germany". *Journal for International Migration and Integration* (2012), DOI: 10.1007/s12134-012-0251-7.

Halm, D. and M. Sauer. "Islamische Gemeinden in Deutschland. Strukturen und Angebote". *Leviathan – Berliner Zeitschrift für Sozialwissenschaft* 40, no. 1 (2012): 71–108.

Halm, D., P. Pielage, L. Pries, T. Tuncay-Zengingül and Z. Sezgin. "Polish and Turkish Migrant Organizations in Germany". In *Cross-Border Migrant Organizations in Comparative Perspective*, edited by L. Pries and Z. Sezgin: 37–98. Basingstoke: Palgrave Macmillan, 2012.

Haug, S., S. Müssig and A. Stichs. *Muslimisches Leben in Deutschland. BAMF Forschungsbericht 6*. Nürnberg: Federal Office for Migration and Refugees (BAMF), 2009.

Klinkhammer, G. *Moderne Formen islamischer Lebensführung. Eine qualitativ-empirische Untersuchung zur Religiosität sunnitisch geprägter Türkinnen der zweiten Generation in Deutschland*. Marburg: Diagonal Verlag, 2000.

Rosenow, K. "Von der Konsolidierung zur Erneuerung – Eine organisationssoziologische Analyse der Türkisch-Islamischen Union der Anstalt für Religion e.V. (DITIB)". In *Jenseits von "Identität oder Integration": Grenzen überspannende Migrantenorganisationen*, edited by L. Pries and Z. Sezgin: 169–200. Wiesbaden: VS Verlag für Sozialwissenschaften, 2010.

Schiffauer, W. *Parallelgesellschaften. Wie viel Wertekonsens braucht unsere Gesellschaft? Für eine kluge Politik der Differenz*. Bielefeld: Transcript, 2008.

Sökefeld, M. "Difficult Identifications: The Debate on Alevism and Islam in Germany". In *Islam and Muslims in Germany*, edited by A. Al-Harmaneh and J. Thielmann: 267–97. Leiden: Brill, 2008.

Thielmann, J. "Vielfältige muslimische Religiosität in Deutschland. Ein Gesamtüberblick zu den Ergebnissen der Studie der Bertelsmann-Stiftung". In *Religionsmonitor 2008. Muslimische Religiosität in Deutschland*. Gütersloh: Bertelsmann Stiftung, 2008.

Thränhardt, D. *Selbstorganisationen von Migrantinnen und Migranten in NRW – Wissenschaftliche Bestandsaufnahme. Schriftenreihe des MASSKS NRW*. Düsseldorf: Ministerium für Arbeit, Soziales und Stadtentwicklung, Kultur und Sport des Landes Nordrhein-Westfalen, 1999.

Tietze, N. *Islamische Identitäten. Formen muslimischer Religiosität bei jungen Männern in Deutschland und Frankreich*. Hamburg: Hamburger Edition, 2001.

Muslims in Italy: The Need for an 'Intesa' with the Italian State

Karim Mezran

Muslims in Italy are now a consistent, although not new, phenomenon in the social and political panorama of the country. Like other communities, they are in search of an agreement with the state that would allow them to live and prosper within a legal framework that guarantees rights and duties. Unfortunately, attempts at achieving such an agreement have come up against a wall of prejudice and fear from the Italian population, as well as a lack of courage and foresight on the part of Italian state institutions. The problems and difficulties associated with the struggle of Italian Muslims in reaching an intesa are outlined and analytically presented along with a discussion of how integration may lead to the type of pluralism and tolerance enshrined in the Italian constitution.

From a historical perspective, Islam's presence in Italy is less a new phenomenon than a 'return' to an earlier era.[1] The Italian peninsula has been subject to Islamic influence since the seventh century, first through acts of piracy from North Africa and later through the Muslim conquest of Sicily and some other enclaves in southern Italy.[2] The Islamic presence in Italy continued throughout the Middle Ages with the trade between Italy and North Africa; thus the language and culture of Italy were also affected by the Islamic influence.

In the period in which Italians conquered part of the territory known today as Libya (1911–42), Italians again came into contact with Muslims. Mussolini, in particular, showed interest in playing a role in the Islamic world. He tried to tie the Italian identity to the Muslim one, arrogated for himself the title of the "Sword of Islam" and, in an important speech before parliament in 1928, defined Italy as a

---

[1] Allievi, "Islam in Italy", 78.
[2] Roggero, "Muslims in Italy", 131.

'Muslim power'. But this attempt to familiarise Italy with Islam only involved the elite and never spilled down to the masses, who remained mostly ignorant of and indifferent to the religion and culture of Muslims.

Islam has thus only recently become an issue in the everyday life of the Italian people. In fact, unlike other European countries, such as France and England, Italy became a destination country for Muslim immigrants relatively late, long after the Second World War, with Muslim immigration only becoming visible in the late 1980s.

This article will, therefore, focus its attention on the phenomenon of Muslim immigration towards Italy in the last two decades and the struggle for the creation of legal norms for the Muslim community in Italy.

In the last decade, especially after the tragic events of 9/11 in New York and the following attacks in London and Madrid, there has been a palpable increase in xenophobia, and Islamophobia in particular, throughout Italy.[3] These feelings are fostered by the political interests of particular parties and by an often ignorant and ill-motivated press. Thus, there is a sense of urgency to find common ground between the two communities with the understanding that the longer this state of affairs – marked by a lack of recognition and cooperation at the socio-political level – continues, the more embittered the Islamic community is likely to become, and the more xenophobic the Italian community.

The first part of this article explains the main characteristics of Italian Islam and Islam in Italy; the second part then discusses the reactions within Italian society at both the social and the political level, thereby singling out the most common factors of friction between the Islamic communities and Italian society. As will be demonstrated, integration processes are never easy, and the Italian case is no exception.

Muslim immigrants in Italy

Before the 1980s, waves of Muslim immigration were directed mainly towards other European countries, such as France, England and Germany. The first two received immigrants mostly from their former colonies: in the case of Great Britain, from Pakistan; in France, from Algeria and Morocco. In the case of Germany, immigrants came principally from Turkey. In general, Muslim immigration in these countries, unlike in Italy, was rather homogeneous in nature.

Italy's Muslim population has expanded rapidly over the past twenty years. According to official data, in 1992 there were about 304,000 Muslims in Italy, a number that increased to 436,000 in 1998.[4] In 2002 it was estimated that the total

---

[3] J. Meletti, "I Guerrieri delle Banlieu, giovani, stranieri e soli", *La Repubblica*, 12 May 2010.
[4] Caritas, *Dossier Caritas Migrantes 2003*, http://www.caritasitaliana.it/pls/caritasitaliana/consultazione. mostra_pagina?id_pagina=405.

number of Muslims in Italy, predominantly Sunni, had increased to 600,000, including 7000 to 10,000 Italian converts.[5] According to the 2008 edition of the *Dossier Caritas Migrantes,* the number of Muslims in Italy had reached 1,253,000 individuals, while the *Lega Musulmana Mondiale* (Muslim World League) puts the number at around 1,200,000.[6] Accordingly, the Muslim community represents about 33 percent of the immigrant population in Italy and around 2 percent of the total Italian population.[7]

Of note is that other dossiers report around 800,000 Muslims in Italy, with the difference in numbers stemming partially from different definitions of 'Muslims', as well as from the fact that some estimates take into consideration both legal and illegal residents (gauged at about 132,000), while others do not. Regarding geographical distribution, about one half of Italian Muslims live in Northern Italy, 30 percent reside in Central Italy, and the rest are in Southern Italy and on the islands. What is certain is that the Islamic presence in Italy has increased significantly in the last twenty years, and that, as a result, Islam has become the country's second religion.

Unlike in other European countries, Muslims in Italy come from at least nine main countries: Morocco, Albania, Tunisia, Senegal, Egypt, Algeria, Pakistan, Bangladesh and Somalia. The greatest number of immigrants comes from Morocco. Moroccans, as well as Tunisians and Albanians, generally perceive Italy not as a transitory country but rather as a country in which they can put down roots. To this end, immigrants from these countries tend to favour family reunification, and often integrate their children by sending them to Italian public schools.

Stefano Allievi identifies the characteristics that distinguish the Muslim immigrant community in Italy from that of other European countries:

- Very recent arrival of immigrants
- Diversity of countries of origin
- Rapid pace of entry and settlement
- Higher number of irregular immigrants
- Higher level of geographic dispersion.

Muslims in Italy are still mostly 'first generation' and are thus more comfortable in their mother tongue than in Italian and more rooted in their home traditions. It is, in the words of the eminent scholar of Muslim immigration in Italy, an Islam *"voltato all'indietro"* (backward looking),[8] and thus not entirely focused on 'integration' which is, on the other hand, its natural destiny.

---

[5] *Ibid.*
[6] Caritas, *Dossier Caritas Migrantes 2008*, http://www.caritasitaliana.it/pls/caritasitaliana/v3_s2ew_consultazione.mostra_pagina?id_pagina=1090.
[7] Toronto, "Islam Italiano", 62.
[8] Allievi, *I Nuovi Musulmani*, 45.

As a consequence of their relatively late arrival, these immigrants also come from countries in which political Islam has already become a central item in the construction of the political-religious and cultural environment. By contrast, immigrants that came to Europe in the late 1960s and 1970s were not affected by the re-Islamisation of the public space in their home countries. Also, given that Italian Muslims come from many different countries, no single ethnic group dominates the Muslim community; Islam in Italy, in other words, cannot be identified with any particular country or region. This makes it harder to treat the Muslim presence in Italy in terms of foreign policy instruments as other European countries tend to do. Since the largest percentage of Muslim immigrants in France comes from Algeria, and in Germany from Turkey, these host countries can try to deal with their immigrants through diplomatic channels with the home countries, whereas the Italians cannot. There are also no major centres of concentration of immigrant communities or Muslim 'ghettos'.

What does it mean to be a Muslim in Italy today?

Roberto Gritti and Magdi Allam came up with a useful categorisation in their study *Islam, Italia* to explain the variety of Islamic beliefs in Italy today.[9] According to this study, Muslims in Italy interpret their faith in one of the following ways:

- *Secular Islam:* Most would consider this the prevailing form in Italy. The majority of Muslim immigrants do not pray regularly, only go to the mosque for festivities and consider integration in European society as a priority. This form of Islam also prevails among those who have converted in order to marry a Muslim.
- *'Ecumenical' Islam:* This form of Islam believes in the parity of Islam with the other monotheist religions. It is committed to the search for common values among Islam, Christianity and Judaism. It is the form of Islam to which the Italian converts adhere most frequently.[10]
- *'Apolitical' Islam:* This group believes in the primacy of faith and excludes any project of a political nature. In Italy, this form of Islam is widespread among Moroccans and Pakistanis who follow the *Jama'at al-Dawa wal Tabligh* (in Italian known as the *Organizzazione dell'Appello e dell'Annuncio*, the Society for the spreading of the faith).
- *Orthodox Islam:* In this group, Muslims pray every day and regularly attend a mosque. This form of Islam is represented in Italy by the *Lega Islamica Mondiale* (*Rabita al Alam al Islami*, Muslim World League), an organisation sponsored by Saudi Arabia.

---

[9] Gritti and Allam, *Islam, Italia.*
[10] On Italian converts in particular, see Allievi, *I Nuovi Musulmani.*

- *Fundamentalist Islam:* This form of Islam aims at Islamising the entire society and embraces both religious and political components. Its strategy is one of Islamisation from below by appealing to the needs of Muslims living in Italy. This group is represented mainly by the *Unione delle Comunità e Organizzazioni Islamiche in Italia* (UCOII, Union of Islamic Communities and Organisations in Italy).

- *Revolutionary Islam:* This is the Islam of the *jihad*. It is the only form of Islam averse to the integration of Muslim immigrants in Italian society.

Given this variety of beliefs or approaches, it is small wonder that the Islamic community in Italy is so weak. It should be noted that the absence in Islam of fixed hierarchies and institutions comparable to Christian churches makes it inherently less compact. That said, this weakness is particularly noticeable in the Italian context, where it is heightened by the aforementioned fragmentation.

In spite of this lack of unity, the many institutions and associations that have been created to represent Muslims in Italy all claim to represent Italian Muslims in their entirety. None of them, however, have ever really succeeded in becoming the 'voice' of Italian Muslims. Moreover, despite intense contacts between these Islamic institutions and Italian institutions, none of them has managed to build a relationship that allows them to be considered the main representative of the Islamic community.

In reality, the only recognised Islamic institution in Italy is the *Centro Islamico Culturale d'Italia* (CICI, Islamic Cultural Centre of Italy), which dates back to 1966. This organisation is run by a group of ambassadors from different Islamic countries. As its financing and management are determined by official state representatives, it is considered an 'Islam of the states'. The centre is linked to the Muslim World League, known for its ties to Saudi Arabia. The most notable project that the *Centro Islamico* has carried out is the building of the Mosque of Monte Antenne in Rome, inaugurated in 1995. The mosque is one of the biggest in Europe and was built with the approval of the Vatican and thanks to the economic contribution of Saudi Arabia.

Another well known Islamic group in Italy is the Union of Islamic Communities and Organisations in Italy, UCOII. This association is the product of the fusion of various previously existing organisations, such as the Syrian and Palestinian components of the *Unione Studenti Musulmani in Italia* (USMI, Union of Muslim Students in Italy), and some Islamic women's organisations, such as *Islam Donne* (Islam Women), with the contribution of some individuals such as Hamza Roberto Piccardo, Italian convert to Islam and former militant of the extremist left-wing movement, *Autonomia Operaia* (Worker Autonomy).[11] UCOII is not only the

---

[11] Piccardo is currently the director of the publishing house Libreriaislamica.it, also known as *Al Hikma* (Allievi, "Islam Italiano e Società Nazionale", 43-75). For a more thorough description of the main journals, organisations and associations on Islam, see Allievi and Dassetto, *Il Ritorno dell'Islam*, and Guolo, *Xenofobi e Xenofili.*

largest organisation in the Islamic community but it also takes pride in being regarded as the most 'democratic'. The workings of its ruling General Assembly are often open to the public. During the recent elections for the leadership of the organisation, Izzeddine el-Zir was elected president and the Italian convert, Alessandro Paolantoni, secretary general.

A third Islamic group of importance is Co.Re.Is, *Comunità Religiosa Islamica Italiana* (Italian Islamic Religious Community) based in Milan. The group was founded by Abdal Wahid Pallavicini and is today led by his son, Sergio Yahya Pallavicini, who is also the *imam* of this community, which consists almost entirely of Italian converts. This religious community is very active in cultural programs such as conferences, seminars and courses. It strives to be the main representative of 'Italian' Islam, but as such it has no substantial relations or ties to the immigrant world.

Alongside these main groups, many others are active in Italy, among them are:

- ACMID (*Associazione comunità marocchina delle donne in Italia*, Association of the Moroccan women's community in Italy), born thanks to the initiative of Suad Sbai, a woman of Moroccan origin and today the only Muslim elected to the Italian parliament within the lists of the centre-right coalition. This organisation is mostly non-religious, but very involved in social issues.
- UMI (*Unione Musulmani Italiani*, Union of Italian Muslims), founded by Abdelaziz Khounati, imam of the *Moschea della Pace* (Mosque of Peace) in Turin. This organisation takes inspiration from a Moroccan political party, *Adala wa Tanmiya* (Development and Justice).
- GMI (*Giovani Musulmani Italiani*, Young Italian Muslims), a group founded in 2001 by young people (14–30 years old) of Islamic origin, who want to integrate in Italian society.[12]

It goes without saying that all these organisations represent a minority of Muslims in Italy. The vast majority, for many reasons, including logistics, do not attend mosques and do not participate in formal organisations. This complicates the issue of integration a great deal and forces one to question the representativeness of Muslim organisations. Simply put, the fact that participation is low and these organisations are not representative of the community presents a major obstacle for reaching an *intesa* with the Italian state (a formal agreement with the state through which the legal rights of a religion are set out).

Representativeness and recognition

All the above-mentioned organisations, as well as many others, struggle to operate in an environment in which there is no clear legal and institutional framework.

---

[12] Frisina, *Giovani Musulmani d'Italia.*

The problem is that, unlike other religious communities, the Muslim community is not a signatory to any intesa.[13]

Italy, like Spain and Portugal, operates under a *concordat* system, a legal system based on the signing of agreements that govern the relations between the state and the religious groups in the country. Several developments in the post-World War II period brought about "a process of deregulation and liberalization in the religious arena" in Italy.[14] The 1947 Italian constitution recognised the previous privileged relations with the Roman Catholic Church (Lateran Treaty, 1929), but also "abolished vestiges of religious discrimination and stipulated that all religions would have equal legal standing".[15]

In 1984, the Italian state decided to renegotiate its concordat with the Catholic Church, removing the Catholic clergy from the state payroll. This coincided with the introduction of the so-called *otto per mille*, by which Italian citizens are required to allocate 0.8 percent of their taxes to either some religious or cultural organisation of their choice or, by default, to the state. Thereafter, in 1993, Italy negotiated an intesa with a non-Catholic church, the Waldensian Church. Agreements with other religious minorities followed: with the Assemblies of God and Seventh-Day Adventists in 1988, with the Union of Jewish Communities in 1989, with the Baptists and Lutherans in 1995. Agreements have also been signed with the Union of Italian Buddhists (1999) and with the Jehova's Witnesses (2000), though these last two have not yet received the needed parliamentary ratification. As Ahmed Vincenzo explains, the intesa has proven to be an important instrument, allowing the religious minorities that live in Italy to be fully recognised and free to enjoy their religious freedoms.[16]

There are many reasons why the Islamic community has failed to reach its aim of signing such an intesa. The principal reason is the rivalry between the various Islamic communities (and their leaders) in Italy, each one of them with a completely different vision, purpose and *modus operandi*. While it is not compulsory for the state to deal exclusively with recognised representatives of the whole community in drafting an intesa, and could in theory sign – as the German state does – different agreements with various representative associations and organisations of the same religious community, this is not the road that the Italian state has decided to pursue.

The state's refusal to deal individually with different groups within the Muslim community has largely been a political issue. In particular, and especially after 9/11, fear of Islamic terrorism, coupled with the rise of Islamophobia in the

---

[13] On this issue in particular, see Casuscelli, "La rappresentanza e l'intesa".

[14] Toronto, "Islam Italiano", 67.

[15] *Ibid.*, 67.

[16] Ahmed Vincenzo is a member of the General Assembly of the Mosque of Monte Antenne in Rome and president of the *Intellettuali Musulmani Italiani* (Italian Muslim Intellectuals) Association. Personal interview, Rome, 22 February 2010.

country, made the state institutions wary of cooperating with organisations affiliated with international Muslim groups such as the Muslim Brotherhood, seen as a radical extremist organisation. Because of this fear and much ignorance regarding the true content of Italian Islam, the state found it safer to deal with these groups informally without granting any particular one the legitimacy of full representativeness of Muslims in Italy.

Throughout the 1990s, attempts were made to reach an intesa: three drafts were produced and presented to the various Italian governments by four Muslim groups. Two of these groups were founded by and are chiefly composed of Italian converts: the *Associazione Musulmani Italiani* (AMI, Association of Italian Muslims, proposal put forth in 1993) and the Co.Re.Is (proposal issued in 1998). The other one is the UCOII (proposal made in 1992). A fourth Islamic body, the CICI, also repeatedly asked for an intesa without, however, proposing a draft version until 2010. In 1998, and again in 2000, the UCOII, the Muslim World League and the CICI established the *Consiglio Islamico d'Italia* (Italian Islamic Council) with the aim of reaching an intesa with the Italian state. But the *Consiglio* was short-lived due to the rivalries between its members: mainly the representatives of the Great Mosque and the UCOII.[17]

All these attempts came to no avail. The UCOII was not granted legal recognition because it was seen as the Italian representative of the Muslim Brotherhood, which at the time was perceived as a radical Islamist organisation. The Co.Re.Is' bid proved to be equally fruitless due to the relatively modest dimensions of the organisation. The reasons for the failure of the proposal of the CICI are unknown to this day, but likely lie in the rivalry with the other organisations as well as the timidity of government institutions, which tend to be very careful not to upset the balance of powers within and between the various religious communities.

In 2005, the Minister of the Interior, Giuseppe Pisanu, established the *Consulta per l'Islam Italiano* (Conference for Italian Islam) made up of sixteen members, half of them Italians, plus other representatives of the UCOII, Co.Re.Is, *Unione Islamica in Occidente* (UIO, Islamic Union in the West), the Muslim World League and the *Comunità Ismailita Italiana* (Italian Ishmaelite Community, a Shi'ite organisation). The Consulta seemed to be based on a compromise between the Italian state, some existing Italian Muslim associations (or, more precisely, those associations that were deemed by the organs of the state as being 'representative' of the Muslim community and thus able to negotiate with the state), and some relevant Muslim countries. It was an attempt to create an institution in which eminent members of the community and leaders of the main organisations could gather together with Italian officials to debate issues, discuss opinions and elaborate proposals to be presented to the Italian parliament for legislative action. It was an

---

[17] Laurence, *Knocking on Europe's Door.*

inclusive and engaging endeavour that was supposed, eventually, to give birth to a common organisation representative of the whole Muslim community.

The aim of the Consulta was never that of reaching an intesa, but rather providing the Minister of the Interior with an interlocutor in the growing religious community with which there would otherwise be no dialogue. The Consulta vaguely resembled a 2003 French experiment: it was expected to work as a consultative body and to include 'moderate' Muslims only – that is, individuals personally chosen by the Minister willing to cooperate with the government.

For various reasons even this initiative failed; continuous infighting between its members on the one hand, and the fact that the new Minister of the Interior of the Berlusconi government, Roberto Maroni, was markedly less interested than his predecessors in the Consulta, ultimately led to its failure. It is evident that a successful Consulta could have, willy nilly, laid the groundwork for a future intesa. As many experts of Islam in Italy have pointed out, an intesa is a *conditio sine qua non* for overcoming many issues linked to the integration process: if it existed, many concerns, such as those discussed in the next section would have been avoided, or at least would seem less important.[18] An intesa in fact would allow the Muslim community to have legitimate and legal representation of its claims before the state; the state would also benefit from having a representative of the second largest religion with whom to dialogue and interact. It would therefore facilitate solutions for many of the ongoing controversies between Muslims and the Italian state.

Despite these obvious benefits to both parties – the Muslim community and the state – the search for an agreement between Islam and the Italian state has reached a standstill. The Muslim community is as fragmented as ever and the rise of xenophobia and anti-Muslim sentiments in the country is paralysing possible initiatives of the state.[19] Furthermore, the state is as shy as ever in approaching the issue of an official intesa with Muslim organisations because of concerns that they will turn out to be fundamentalist.

In February 2010, after more than a year of silence, the public was informed by a note from the Ministry of the Interior that a new body, the *Comitato per l'Islam Italiano* (Committee for Italian Islam) had been formed by then-Interior Minister Roberto Maroni. It was supposed to take the place of the Consulta, the organisation formed by the previous ministers Pisanu and Giulio Amato. Unfortunately, however, Minister Maroni's Comitato was a step backward from the more inclusive and collaborative Consulta.

As Maroni himself explained, while the Consulta was supposed to represent the whole of the Islamic world in Italy, even though it clearly had no official representatives, the new body is simply a group of people that know the Muslim world

---

[18] L. Manconi, "Diritti e Doveri degli Islamici d'Italia", *Corriere della Sera,* 28 August 2002.
[19] V. Polchi, "Imam d'Italia. Chi comanda nelle Moschee", *La Repubblica*, 8 February 2010, 23.

well and are integrated in Italian society. Many members of the Muslim community suspected that the government was choosing its 'loyal' Muslims in order to provide a fig leaf for its anti-Islamic policies, especially those leading to decisions regarding the two essential issues discussed below: the building of new mosques and the appointment and training of imams.[20]

Controversies between Muslims and the Italian state, and the role of the media

The rivalry between Muslim organisations does not belie the existence of many points of controversy between Italy's Islamic communities and the Italian state. In particular the Muslim side has raised concern regarding the following issues:

- women's right to wear the *hijab;*
- the presence of the crucifix and other Christian symbols in public places (schools, offices, etc.);
- the right to a *halal* menu in the refectories;
- legal recognition of polygamous marriages;
- the right to 'practice' Islamic butchering;
- the right to study Islamic books coming from the Muslim world (Saudi Arabia) in private Islamic schools;
- the right to build new mosques.

Of all these requests, the most discussed and the one that has heated the debate and the political climate the most concerns the right to build new places of worship. It is evident that this difficult and painful issue can only be overcome through legal recognition of the Muslim community. Legal recognition would provide all the rights and possibilities given other religious communities as well as all the duties that follow. Nevertheless, the situation is particularly bad. In 2009, an investigative report published in one of the most prominent Italian weeklies, *L'Espresso*, showed that an 'invisible Islam' is spreading throughout the country.[21] Indeed, there are an estimated 749 'Islamic worship places' in Italy, but less than a handful of them are real mosques. Ninety-nine percent of them are illegal in the sense that they do not comply with standard regulations regarding health and safety in public spaces (most have, for example, neither emergency exits nor access to regular toilets). Apart from the Mosque of Monte Antenne in Rome, the one in Milano Segrate, and the Catania Mosque inaugurated in 1980 and later privatised and closed to the public, and a few Islamic centres (Trent, Naples and Turin), the other places are simply garages, warehouses and sheds. Muslims in Italy, in the

---

[20] Personal interview by author with imams and members of Islamic community in Rome, Turin and Milan, 2010.
[21] Biondani, "L'Islam Invisibile".

north (Veneto and Lombardy) as well as in the deep south (Sicily, Calabria, Campania) pray in warehouses and abandoned factories or even under tents pitched in fields.

Many problems arise from the existence of these ad hoc mosques. Most notably, the security risk, which derives from the fact that these places cannot be monitored by police and security institutions. Secondly, but just as important, because of the indecency of most of these places of worship, the religious dignity of Muslim immigrants is trampled on. This has often been reported as one of the major causes of alienation and resentment among Muslims towards Italians.

There have been many attempts by radical political forces to limit the building of mosques in Italy in recent years. Following the results of the Swiss referendum on minarets, a new proposal was presented to prohibit the building of a mosque within a thousand meters of a Catholic Church. In Italy, where there is a church on every other street, it goes *sans dire* that the passing of such a proposal would forbid the building of mosques in most parts of the country. Other proposals range from demanding that the building of a new mosque be subject to a referendum by the inhabitants of the city to demanding the appointment of state officials on the board of directors of the new mosques. Unfortunately, the Italian political establishment has yet to realise that by acting in this confused, undecided, and ambiguous way it makes the community operate in a fragmented, opaque, and often clandestine way. Collectively, these harsh conditions and restrictions are more likely to lead to the terrorism the state fears so much than the actual building of new mosques.

Mistrust runs in all directions. In every European country, at least one political party has exploited this widespread discontent and centred the party program on the need to limit the damages caused by immigration. The issue of building new mosques as well as all other issues concerning the Muslim presence in Italy have become so highly politicised that Islamophobia has become one of the main planks – even if not always explicitly – of the platforms of these right-wing parties in Italy.[22] In Italy this role appertains to the *Lega Nord* (Northern League), a political party popular in Northern Italy. It is nationalistic, xenophobic and separatist in orientation. The Lega Nord has tried to tap into the various resentments expressed at the popular level against the "large number of immigrants" who "pollute the streets, create disorder and commit crimes", and use it for political gain. For these parties, verbally, and sometimes physically, attacking Muslim immigrants and contrasting the expansion of their symbols (mosques, traditional dress, typical stores and restaurants) has paid off, at least in terms of popularity and votes.[23]

Another important issue concerns the mosque preachers and leaders, the so-called imams. Frequently, on television and in the newspapers, imams are accused

---

[22] Guolo, *Xenofobi e Xenofili.*
[23] Lucassen and Lubbers, "Who Fears What?", 547.

of supporting Islamic radicalism and inciting the faithful to violence. This has led to the request that the state organise the appointment of Muslim preachers and community leaders. Until today, no agreement has been reached on this point. There has been much discussion on allowing Italian universities to create faculties of Islamic culture in order to prepare teachers and preachers for the Islamic religion. This could be a good avenue if done in collaboration with moderate Muslim organisations and perhaps foreign Muslim institutions of high standing. But on this point as well no definitive consensus has been reached.

The truth is that most imams, particularly those in Italy's rundown mosques, are not sent by Islamic transnational or official religious institutions, nor are they sent by the Ministry for Religious Education of any Muslim state. They are simply individuals, often without any background in religious studies, who emerge in a position of leadership in their communities due to their support for traditions and traditional customs. That is why these imams, unlike those in the Middle East, often become spokespersons for their communities and are often called on to interact with official Italian institutions. It is evident that this state of affairs cannot continue as such. Some intervention is needed, and not only for security reasons.

Moreover, the media tends to be superficial in treating news related to Muslims in Italy, thus enhancing misperception and bias. Some newspapers publish opinions that are highly inflammatory and aggressive. A good example is the opinion represented by the eminent political scientist Giovanni Sartori, long-time professor at Columbia University and frequent guest on television shows discussing important political issues. Particularly shocking was an article of his published on the first page of the prominent daily newspaper *Corriere della Sera* in December 2009. In this article, entitled "The Integration of Muslims", this important opinion-maker explicitly stated the "impossibility of the integration of Muslims in 'any' European country". After a historical overview of the incompatibility of this community with others, unlike the Chinese, Indians and Japanese who, for example, have integrated smoothly everywhere while keeping their cultural and religious identities, Sartori explained why this will not happen with Muslims. "Islam is not a domestic religion; it is an invasive theocratic monotheism that after a long period of stagnation has reawakened and is inflammatory. It is an illusion to think that it can be integrated by Italianising it, this is a risk taken by naïve people, a risk not to be risked."[24] Fortunately, much can be done by Italian converts and by second generation Muslim immigrants who know both cultures and are determined to find their place within Italian society. According to Annalisa Frisina, an Italian scholar who has devoted many studies to the analysis of second generation Muslim

---

[24] G. Sartori, "L'integrazione e gli Islamici", *Corriere della Sera*, 20 December 2009. See also his rebuttal to reactions to the original article, "Una Replica ai Pensabenisti sull''Islam", *Corriere della Sera*, 5 January 2010.

immigrants, these individuals do not try to promote religion *per se* but work to develop an identity that can fit the realities of Italian life. These second generation Muslims have greater ambitions than their fathers and want to be recognised as full citizens of the Islamic faith. They struggle for the realisation of an Islam that is 'Italian', and prefer to speak, discuss and write in Italian, unlike the leaders of the first generation who almost always resorted to Arabic or their own native language. It is evident that through their initiatives new avenues for Muslim participation in Italian socio-political life can be devised.

Conclusion

Though Italian Islam shares many issues prevalent within European Islam, it has many peculiarities: partly because it is in its infancy, partly because Muslim immigrants in Italy are a heterogeneous group. As such, it is impossible to draw consistent conclusions about the community or make predictions about the direction that its interaction with the Italian people and state will take. Thus, this article has been limited to an analysis of how Muslims have tried to integrate themselves in Italian politics and how the Italians have reacted to a Muslim presence in their country.

Muslim communities in Italy, moreover, differ in principles and *modi operandi*. Partially as a result of this, their dialogue with Italian society has not been very profitable thus far. While Italian society has often proven to be biased towards immigrants in general and Muslims in particular,[25] a lack of legal recognition of the Muslim community in Italy has further embittered the dialogue. This state of limbo exacerbates the already deep divisions within the Muslim community and its political and religious organisations, which contributes to the creation of conflicts and animosity.

If the Muslim associations in Italy were to speak with a single voice, and if Italian politics were less near-sighted, the situation would certainly improve. It is essential, at this critical socio-political juncture, that all parties concerned begin thinking about the Muslim issue as a 'normal' issue; in practical terms, this means treating the Muslim community like other immigrant and/or religious communities, rather than an 'exceptional' one to be dealt with differently and through different means. Therefore, what is needed is a normalisation of relations and, more importantly, the realisation of a regulatory structure for them.

As for every other social or political alteration, a society needs some time to accept change and to consider the new situation as a normality; time will have to pass before Muslims feel at home in Italy. Nevertheless, the march in this direction has begun and will be carried forward, as " . . . it is clear that integration of Muslims

---

[25] Allievi, "Islam Italiano e Società Nazionale", 59.

will gradually become a reality, and Italian society and the Islamic community will be permanently changed in the process".[26]

References

Allievi, S. "Islam Italiano e Società Nazionale". In *Islam in Europa/Islam in Italia. Tra Diritto e Società*, edited by A. Ferrari: 43–77. Bologna: il Mulino, 2008.

Allievi, S. "Islam in Italy". In *Islam. Europe's Second Religion*, edited by S.T. Hunter: 77–95. London: Praeger, 2002.

Allievi, S. *I Nuovi Musulmani. I Convertiti all'Islam*. Rome: Edizioni Lavoro, 1999.

Allievi, S. and F. Dassetto. *Il Ritorno dell'Islam. I musulmani in Italia*. Rome: Edizioni Lavoro, 1993.

Biondani, P. "L'Islam Invisibile". *L'Espresso* 43 (29 October 2009): 60–3.

Caritas. *Dossier Caritas-Migrantes*. Rome: Edizioni Idos, 2003 and 2008.

Casuscelli, G. "La rappresentanza e l'intesa". In *Islam in Europa/Islam in Italia. Tra Diritto e Società*, edited by A. Ferrari: 285–325. Bologna: il Mulino, 2008.

Frisina, A. *Giovani Musulmani d'Italia*. Rome: Carocci editore, 2007.

Gritti, R. and M. Allam. *Islam, Italia: Chi sono e cosa pensano i musulmani che vivono tra noi*. Milan: Guerini e Associati, 2001.

Guolo, R. *Xenofobi e Xenofili. Gli Italiani e l'Islam*. Rome, Bari: Laterza, 2003.

Laurence, J. *Knocking on Europe's Door: Islam in Italy, Brookings US-Europe Analysis no. 27*. Washington, DC: Brookings Institution, February 2006.

Lucassen, G. and M. Lubbers. "Who Fears What? Explaining Far-Right-Wing Preference in Europe by Distinguishing Perceived Cultural and Economic Ethnic Threats". *Comparative Political Studies* 45, no. 5 (2012).

Roggero, M. A. "Muslims in Italy". In *Muslims in the West, From Sojourners to Citizens*, edited by Y. Yazbeck Haddad: 131–43. Oxford: Oxford University Press, 2002.

Toronto, J. "Islam Italiano: Prospects for Integration of Muslims in Italy's Religious Landscape". *Journal of Muslim Minority Affairs* 28, no. 1 (April 2008): 61–82.

---

[26] Toronto, "Islam Italiano", 79.

The Netherlands and Islam: In Defence of Liberalism and Progress?

Saskia van Genugten

With the elections of 2012, the main party driving the Islam debate in the Netherlands was sidelined. The new government of Liberals and Social Democrats is trying to re-bury the contentious issue, not least because Islam-related questions have had a confusing effect on their parties. Nonetheless, with societal concerns lingering, the topic is likely to reappear. In the Netherlands, the wariness towards (Islamic) immigration is not rooted in fears of ethnic or religious competition. Instead, it tends to receive serious political attention only when cloaked as a defence of secularist and liberal values. As such, curbing Islamic practices is presented as a way to protect a (self-promoted) image of the Netherlands as a non-judgemental and tolerant place. The paradox remains that that self-image was traditionally meant to include minorities, not to exclude them.

The Dutch general elections of 12 September 2012 saw two main winners: the Liberal and the Labour parties. Geert Wilders' Freedom Party (PVV) was quickly identified as the biggest loser. During his campaign in this last election, Wilders had prioritized anti-Europeanism over anti-immigration. Compounded by internal discord within his party's ranks, this resulted in a loss of 9 seats in the Lower House, leaving him with a rather insignificant 15 seats (out of 150) in the new political constellation. The winners quickly went on to sideline his party. During his visit to Ankara in early November 2012, Prime Minister Mark Rutte told his Turkish interlocutors to "forget about Wilders".[1] According to the new coalition, the chapter of experimenting with populism in Dutch politics, has been closed.

The outcome of the elections could indeed suggest a return to 'normality'; a revival of consensual politics of the middle, in which populist forces are effortlessly exposed as unreliable and obstructive. One could interpret this as an end to a

---

[1] See, for example, "Zet Wilders uit jullie hoofd", *Trouw*, 7 November 2012.

decade of immigration fury and soul-searching that started with the unprecedented rise of Wilders' predecessor, Pim Fortuyn. Bills aimed at banning the burqa and prohibiting ritual slaughtering have stalled. The abolition of the Minister for Immigration, Integration and Asylum is a symbolic statement by Liberals and Labour that in this direction also, a chapter has been closed.

But the latest developments can also be interpreted as a truce, enforced by the economic crisis. The current collaboration of Liberals and Labour is an attempt to foster consensus and to provide the Netherlands, after a decade of turmoil, with a stable political outlook – one of the prerequisites for overcoming the crisis. For the moment, contentious issues such as the integration of Muslim practices into Dutch society are judged of inferior importance. Even when not mentioned as explicitly as before, matters related to immigration and Islam remain of relevance. In the last decade, (Islamic) immigration was launched rapidly to the top of the political agenda – reflecting lingering societal concerns. As these concerns remain, the issue will most likely reappear. In comparison to a decade ago, immigration and integration policies have become far stricter and taboos with regard to Islam have been shattered. Wilders' Freedom Party may have lost its appeal for the moment, but several of his views have been integrated in mainstream political thinking. The new cabinet will continue a tough immigration and integration policy. EU partners will be pressured for stricter rules regarding family reunion and re-admission agreements with third countries. New proposals will be made to ban face-covering clothing from schools, public institutions and public transport. Another proposal targets marriage between cousins.

Upheaval in several party ranks also indicates that the soul-searching within long-established political parties continues. Confronted with questions related to (Islamic) immigration, the traditional parties are forced to slightly (re)interpret their respective dominant worldview – liberalism, socialism or (Christian) confessionalism. Does liberalism have limits? Does liberalism apply to the less-liberal? Does freedom of religion hold for other religions? Even when the other might not grant the same freedoms? Indeed, do we tolerate the intolerant? Does solidarity and the redistribution of welfare apply to newcomers? Also to 'the non-integrated' that do not speak the native language and might send the money directly abroad? In the new coalition agreement, one of the proposals is to deny social assistance to those unable to pass a Dutch language test.

In the following pages, the debate about immigration and Islam in the Netherlands is explored. In particular, the analysis zooms in on the questions of why, in the Netherlands, 'tolerance', 'progress' and 'secular liberal values' have become central tenets of this debate, and not, as for example in Italy, the interaction between Islam and Christianity, or, as in France, the consequences for state secularism. As such, the aim is to highlight some of the idiosyncratic elements of the more general 'Europe and Islam' debate.

The centrality of tolerance, liberalism and secular progress

Since the cultural revolution of the 1960s, the Netherlands likes to be considered a non-judgemental paradise for political, cultural and sexual minorities. The tiny, densely populated and relatively rich country prides itself on its policies based on consensus, compromise and inclusiveness. To analyse the impact of immigration, it makes sense to take a closer look at the reason and the way the Dutch have forged a national image built on far-reaching liberal – some would say libertarian – and progressive values.

Much of it goes back to the consolidation of a national myth and the selection of founding concepts by authorities interested in creating a cohesive feeling – a communal loyalty to the national state.[2] For the Netherlands, 'tolerance for diversity' was singled out as one of the core tenets of its national stereotype. After violent sectarian clashes in the Thirty Year War (1618–48, referred to as the 'Eighty Year War' in Dutch history, lasting from 1568–1648), inhabitants of the Northern European backwater registered that downplaying religious or ethnic differences had a positive effect on economic development and that tolerance could be a driving force of societal progress. Negotiating consensus and cooperation led to economic growth. The authorities encouraged a national image in which giving into strong emotions was regarded as barbarism and exclusive thinking was believed to lead to conflict. Dutch soil was to be praised for its inclusiveness, especially regarding minorities. The nationally acclaimed poet, Jacob Slauerhoff (1898 – 1936), captured this mentality wonderfully in his poem "In the Netherlands".[3]

'Evidence' of such national characteristics was collected throughout history. Often quoted examples include the fact that at the height of the Spanish Inquisition, the Dutch compassionately welcomed Sephardic Jews fleeing the Iberian Peninsula. At the end of the seventeenth century, the Dutch accommodated the French Huguenots and, after World War II, the story of Anne Frank was considered representative for the nation's feelings towards the German-imposed minority policies. More recently, starting in the 1960s, a strong secularisation refocused the 'moral superiority' of the Dutch on new types of minorities, especially all possible sexual minorities. At the international level, the Netherlands – the land of Hugo Grotius – found its calling in depicting itself as the cradle of international justice and the ultimate protector of minorities. The Peace Palace, the International Court of Justice and the more recent proposal to turn Amsterdam into 'Shelter City' for political dissidents all stand witness to this desire to be a 'Guiding Country'.[4]

This externally promoted image of national inclusiveness was elaborated rather differently with regard to societal patterns of behaviour. The social constellation the

---

[2]See, for example, Gellner, *Nations and Nationalism*, and Anderson, *Imagined Communities*.
[3]Slauerhoff, "In Nederland", 337
[4]Referring to the slogan *Nederland Gidsland*, launched in the 1960s and used ever since to reflect the Dutch self-image of a progressive nation. See also van Noort, *Nederland als voorbeeldige natie*.

Dutch authorities initially had to work with was all but cohesive, and the societal structure appeared built around a system known as 'pillarisation'. Catholics, Protestants, Liberals and Socialists moved within their distinctive 'pillars'. Each pillar had its own political party, newspaper, television channel, school, hospital, trade union, sports clubs, etc. Intergroup contacts were judged unnecessary and undesirable. For the individual, there was hardly reason to challenge these divisions – except perhaps when love was at stake. In general, the masses remained compliant and trusted their respective traditional political leaders to do what was best for them.

With regard to the political system, the national myth and particular worldview translated into consensual and inclusive politics of the centre characterizing a so-called 'consociational democracy'.[5] Guaranteed intergroup consultation and inclusive elite-negotiation constitute the core mechanisms of this type of politics. Party competition was kept to a minimum and decisions were ideally based on accommodation and solidarity. Nevertheless, as pointed out in the last paragraph, these *intergroup* elite negotiations were accompanied by strict separation at the level of the masses. Thus, while the concept of tolerance and inclusiveness has often been used for political reasons to define the Dutch *nation* (that is, the people), technically the only tolerant and inclusive ones were the *state institutions*. Tensions have always existed between the self-perception of being tolerant and inclusive and the fact that this tolerance was imposed from above. In fact, at the grass-root level, tolerance was hardly ever seriously tested.

Mass immigration provided the first significant test of this tolerance. In the past decade, many Dutch citizens felt that something 'non-Dutch' was happening to their country. They pointed to several events that shook the country. In 2002, the assassination of politician Pim Fortuyn constituted the first Dutch experience with political murder since the 17th century. Two years later, a group of radical Dutch Muslims subjected the controversial moviemaker Theo van Gogh to an even more gruesome fate, cutting his throat and using a knife to pin a letter to his chest addressed to Ayaan Hirsi Ali, ex-Muslim and back then, Member of the Dutch Lower House. In April 2009, the Queen herself became the target of an attack. She came out unscathed, but five bystanders were killed. To some, the simultaneous rise of anti-immigration parties suggested that immigration, especially from Islamic countries, was a significant factor in these developments.

Of course, immigration constituted just one element of a more complex story that caused confusion. Other factors included a loss of policy control through deregulation and Europeanisation, as well as a loss of faith in political institutions and politicians.[6] The story also involved social media increasing the choices in individual belonging and the further crumbling of traditional 'pillarised'

---

[5]Lijphart, *The Politics of Accommodation*.
[6]"Politicus geniet evenveel vertrouwen als een autoverkoper: vrijwel nul", *De Volkskrant*, 22 August 2012. See also Hendriks, "Contextualizing the Dutch Drop in Political Trust", 473–91.

communities. After the cultural and sexual revolution of the 1960s, linked to rapid secularisation and individualization, these pillars started to become increasingly obsolete. In addition, economic, financial and demographic developments forced citizens to recognise that state solidarity from cradle to grave can no longer be taken for granted. Resources are becoming scarcer, sparking the question of redistribution. And there, full circle, we are back to the issue of immigration and social cohesion.

Mass immigration and de-pillarisation

Up until the 1940s, while divided on Christian doctrines, the Netherlands was an extremely ethnically homogeneous place. Only 1.1 percent of the population had roots outside of its tiny territory. The diversity in worldviews as enhanced by the pillarisation was real, but would also classify for Freud's narcissism of small differences. Questions of *national* identity hardly ever emerged. De-pillarisation took place in conjunction with mass immigration and the discourse changed from one of Catholics, Protestants and secularists to one including a differentiation between *autochtonen* (natives) and *allochtonen* (non-natives). To clarify, in theory and in statistical analyses, somebody is considered *allochtoon* if at least one parent is born abroad. Those born on foreign soil are referred to as first generation *allochtonen*, with a second generation *allochtonen* born on Dutch soil. Statistically speaking, the third generation deserves the label *autochtoon*, but in mainstream discourse this generation keeps being referred to as *allochtoon*.

Large-scale immigration to the Netherlands has two main sources.[7] On the one hand, immigrants arrived from former colonies (especially Indonesia, Suriname and the former Dutch Antilles). On the other hand, the Netherlands witnessed economically motivated immigration from – predominantly – Morocco and Turkey, based on recruitment agreements between the Dutch and the Moroccan and Turkish authorities. Individuals from the first group were considered permanent residents from the start, while those from the second group were initially seen as a temporary exchange of labour. Their permanence only emerged after the oil crises of the 1970s, when single male 'guest workers' brought their families over and Dutch authorities started promoting the concept of a multicultural society. Muslim families created a more distinct profile for themselves and became active in an increasing number of societal arenas, including those of education, health care and social welfare. In 1975, the percentage of 'non-natives' in the total population stood at 9.9 percent. In 2009, this was close to 20 percent, with 'non-Western non-natives' (statistical category) making up 11 percent.

---

[7] For a good overview of the history of Islam in the Netherlands, see Sengers and Sunier, *Religious Newcomers and the Nation-state*.

The following tables give an overview of the growth in absolute numbers of non-natives in the Netherlands (first and second generation) and of the growing percentage of people declaring themselves Muslim in the Netherlands. Statistics on this subject are never perfect. In 2008, around 6 percent of the population (900,000) were estimated to be Muslim.[8] By contrast, in 1971, that estimation was at 50,000.[9] Immigrants with Turkish or Moroccan backgrounds constitute the largest groups, followed by those with roots in Suriname, Afghanistan and Iraq. There are around 12,000 Dutch converts.[10] As in many other European countries, Islam has become the largest non-Christian religion of the Netherlands.

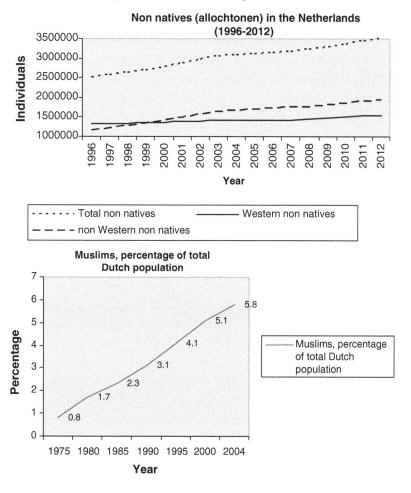

---

[8]Sunier, "Islam in the Netherlands", 115.
[9]CBS Statline (database).
[10]CBS Statline (database).

Integration in state institutions

How tolerant was the Netherlands with regard to the influx of this new religious minority? 'Very tolerant' would be the answer when focusing merely on *state institutions*. The Dutch state does not have an established church and is neutral to all religions. Most basically, Article 1 of the Constitution grants the right to equal treatment and outlaws discrimination on grounds of religion, belief, political opinion, race, sex or any other ground. In addition, Article 6 of the Constitution grants every individual the right to practice his or her religion, individually or within a community, as long as these practices fall within the limits of the law. The state is nonetheless given the authority to intervene, if needed, on grounds of public health or public order.

The existing legal framework turned out to be rather flexible in incorporating Islam. Legal provisions aimed at accommodating more established religions applied to Islam as well, including tax exemptions for religious practices, special arrangements on ritual animal slaughtering, circumcision practices and burial rites.[11] In 1963, a Church Construction Act had made it possible to obtain indirect subsidies to build places of worship.[12] But just when the demand for mosques started to grow rapidly, this Act expired. Judging this a form of indirect discrimination leaving Muslims without the necessary infrastructure to practice their faith, national legislators passed two regulations aimed at providing for mosques.[13] In addition, with mosques traditionally combining social, cultural, educational and religious functions, subsidies could be arranged through cultural and educational funds. As a result, the number of mosques has grown to around 500. Today, some forty Islamic schools are registered, including primary, middle and high schools (which, like all other schools, need to include standard curriculum and are subject to state inspection).[14] Since 1997, Rotterdam hosts an Islamic University. Broadcast rights have been granted to Muslim organisations and Islamic banks and other social infrastructure have also emerged.[15]

Was a small but solid Muslim pillar in the making (while traditional ones were crumbling)? Not really. Behind what could be perceived as a cohesive pillar were a myriad of different forms of religiosity and cultural practices. Those with Turkish,

---

[11]Van Bijsterveld, "The Legal Status of Islam".

[12]A government committee was set up to investigate the issue and the related Waardenburg Working Group advised that the state should subsidize the construction of mosques.

[13]See Van Bijsterveld, "The Legal Status of Islam", 136; and Rath *et al.*, "Islamic Institutions in a De-pillarizing Society", 389–95.

[14]Islamitische Schoolbesturen Organisatie (ISBO), "Islamitisch basisonderwijs in Nederland, ontstaan, organisatie en integratie", http://www.deisbo.nl/wp-content/uploads/2010/03/islamitischonderwijsinnederland.pdf.

[15]The largest ones were "Dutch Muslim Broadcast" and "Dutch Islamic Broadcast", but the organisations were closed down after a series of scandals and a bankruptcy in 2009.

Surinamese, Moroccan and other roots all had their own group dynamics and traditions.[16] This made integration as a group more difficult and raised the question of who to talk to at the national level, a problem encountered in many other European countries.

Integration into the fabric of society

State institutions tended to embrace the newcomers. But at the level of society – of people-to-people contacts – accommodation was less obvious. State institutions encouraged the view of immigration as an abstract cultural enrichment, but many perceived a concrete clash with prevailing norms and values. Full-fledged immigrant families started to make use of the established structures and problems sprang up with regard to daily interactions. For example, parents questioned mixed groups in kindergarten, in gym and swimming classes; some women refused to be treated by a male doctor or always wanted their husband to be present during consultations. Language barriers amplified the complexity and created social miscommunication.

However, understanding was not automatically improved by the tearing down of language barriers and increased dialogue. Actually, a better awareness of certain groups' views on gender equality, homosexuality, sex in general, abortion and euthanasia, led to the question of compatibility of Muslim beliefs with dominant 'Dutch' views on these issues. From the officially encouraged liberal perspective and belief in progress regarding respect for diversity, some of the Muslim immigrants were judged to lag behind, to be stuck in an un-Enlightened 'stage' of community-based thinking, of superstitious, irrational religious behaviour and old-fashioned views.

From that conclusion, two lines of thinking evolved: a majority believed that culture could adapt and that progress would ultimately also touch the Muslim migrant; immigrants would naturally adapt to their new environment. Others started stressing that Islam was different, essentially static and unchangeable. In the latter view, the increasing number of Muslim immigrants would erode the social values and tolerance generated on Dutch soil.

Dutch politics and Islam

In a democracy, politics are a reflection of what society stands for. As outlined before, from the 1960s onwards, the Netherlands witnessed a rapid secularization and individualization. In 1860, the country was still strictly Christian, with 60 percent Protestant, the rest Roman Catholic. In 1899, only 2 percent stated that they did not belong to a certain religious group. In 1960 this was already 18

---

[16]Vink, "Beyond the Pillarization Myth", 337–50.

percent and by 1990 this number had risen to 40 percent.[17] Church attendance dropped dramatically, with religion becoming ever more individualized and privatized. Impositions from central authorities started to lose legitimacy at a similar pace. The first clear reflection at the political level of the crumbling pillars was the successful appearance of a new party, called Democrats '66. This new party played on individualism and secularism. Among other things, it called for increased citizen participation in politics – a public challenge to the mass-elite divide. A second breach of the traditional order came in 1977, with the merger of the Catholic and Protestant parties into one Christian Democratic party (CDA).

The rapid influx of (Islamic) immigrants led to another blow to the traditional political system. Playing on societal unease regarding immigration and Islam would prove a real goldmine for political actors, if approached in the right way. An anti-immigrant party had already been formed in the 1980s. But the Centrum Party (later the Centrum-Democrats) would, at the height of its political success in the early 1990s, capture only 2.4 percent of the vote. Building its narrative on racial and ethnocentric arguments, the party was considered an outlaw, a sort of counter-image of the Dutch psyche. Only when the Liberal politician Frits Bolkestein started questioning the compatibility of Islam with liberal democracy, did a feeling of unease with the newcomers trickle into mainstream politics. Paul Scheffer, a prominent member of the Labour Party, approved of this view and questioned whether Dutch views on Islam and the multicultural society were not too tolerant and accommodating. After all, he stated, with more than 1 million Muslims at home in the near future, one could only hope for a liberal and secularized Islam, but there was no guarantee.[18] To get immigration and Islam truly on the political agenda, a political entrepreneur was needed who would link the issue to another lingering discontent: that of a political elite out of touch with large part of society. Views on immigration were to illustrate the gap between elite and mass perceptions. Indeed, bashing Islamic immigration on ethnocentric grounds had not received much political following, but questioning Islamic immigration framed as a defence of secular and progressive values appealed to a wider electorate.[19]

The politician, Pim Fortuyn, was the first to successfully tap into popular apprehension about immigration and raised Islam to the level of national politics. In 2001, he struck the right chord by directly attacking the, in his opinion, uninformed and paternalistic views of society of the traditional parties.[20] Fortuyn skilfully connected the gap between political leaders and masses with the belief that, while Muslims had been treated as the weaker party or as victims, the real victim

---

[17] Since then, the percentage has stagnated. Schmeets and Van der Bie, *Religie aan begin de 21ste eeuw.*
[18] P. Scheffer, "Het multiculturele drama", *NRC Handelsblad,* 29 January 2000, http://retro.nrc.nl/W2/Lab/Multicultureel/scheffer.html.
[19] Van Bohemen *et al.,* "Seculiere intolerantie", 199–218.
[20] Fortuyn, *De puinhopen van Paars* [The Purple Mess].

was Dutch society and its values of democracy, inclusiveness, freedom of expression, secularism and liberalism. In his words:

> Islam, it isolates people. They see us as an inferior kind of people. Did you notice that Moroccan boys never steal from other Moroccans? But they are allowed to steal from us. And with regard to me, it would count double, as I am not only a Christian dog, but am worth less than a pig [referring to his homosexuality]. If I could make it legally possible, I would simply say: no more Muslims will enter the country! But I cannot do that, legally speaking. But Islam is a backward – I will just say it – it is simply a backward culture.[21]

In the wake of 9/11, in the 2002 general elections, the remnants of Fortuyn's party won 26 out of 150 seats. He himself was assassinated 9 days before the elections. Without his leadership, the party quickly fell apart. But the electorate sensed that, after all, politicians could appeal to the general populace; issues previously considered taboo could finally be raised. For the political establishment itself, the lesson was that immigration, integration and especially Islam had to be taken up as 'problematic issues' on the political agenda.[22] After Fortuyn's breakthrough, Geert Wilders and his Freedom Party (PVV) have been the most successful heirs of this legacy. In the 2010 elections they received 24 seats, 15.4 percent of the votes. Wilders presented Islam not as a religion, but as a dangerous political ideology (and therefore exempt from fundament religious freedoms).[23]

Specific immigration policies had been articulated since the early 1970s. Initially, a somewhat restrictive immigration policy was tried out but soon proven rather pointless in combination with the fundamental right to family life, the legal underpinning of family reunion.[24] In 1979, for the first time, the Scientific Council for Governmental Policy suggested government intervention to prevent socio-economic disadvantages and the cultural isolation of immigrants.[25] In the early 1980s, the government started to describe Dutch society officially as an immigrant society. Accepting the fact of permanency, the focus shifted to integration, though to an integration aimed at preserving different cultural identities. Back then, the general political consensus was one of compatibility between integration and the nurturing of distinct cultural traditions. In the 1980s, the full range of legislation was scrutinized and rid of clauses that were at odds with Article 1 or 6 of the Constitution.[26] In 1986, the Dutch Nationality Act was changed to include *ius soli,* making naturalization less troublesome and obtaining double passports were possible for several years. With all these legal tools, minorities were assumed to

---

[21]F. Poorthuis and H. Wansink, "De Islam is een achterlijke cultuur", *De Volkskrant*, 9 February 2002, http://www.volkskrant.nl/den_haag/article153195.ece/De_islam_is_een_achterlijke_cultuur%C2%A0.
[22]Pelikaan *et al.*, "Fortuyn's Legacy", 282–302.
[23]*Ibid.*
[24] See, for example, the European Convention for Human Rights (ECHR), Article 8.
[25]WRR, *Etnische Minderheden*.
[26]Beune and Hessels, *Minderheid – Minder recht?*

integrate smoothly into the open, tolerant societal space the Netherlands was believed to offer. Society, the assumption was, could be constructed top-down.

But the reality was that the government could only actively and directly implement its envisioned equality and tolerance in the public sector.[27] The private sector often remained at unease with the Islamic newcomers. A poor command of the Dutch language and dress and demands deviating from the norm could negatively impact business images. The government reacted, in 1994, with an Equal Treatment Act and the establishment of an institution to examine cases of direct and indirect discrimination, especially with regard to education and employment. The buzzwords of 'non-discrimination' and 'tolerance' silenced contrary views. The exclamation 'discrimination!' turned into a powerful manipulative instrument of (Muslim) migrants.

Fortuyn's victory exposed the limits of accommodating policies. The initial reaction was to engage – against the advice of the Scientific Council for Governmental Policy – in the construction of a more stringent idea of a Dutch identity. The overall aim was to give non-natives a road map to cultural integration, and perhaps to assert to the natives that they had a national identity to preserve, the tolerant, liberal and progressive one. New guidelines for history textbooks appeared and a plan for a National Historical Museum made headlines. In a contest for the Greatest Dutchman in history, William of Orange (assassinated in 1584) had to share first place with Pim Fortuyn, assassinated not long before the contest. Immigrants were asked to pass a costly exam, including a language and a culture assessment, before being admitted to the Netherlands.[28] Especially the video distributed for the cultural part caused fury. Indirectly, it made a statement of what Dutch national identity, according to the national authorities, should be: the video showed topless women on North Sea beaches and gay couples making out in public under the banner: this is what you should expect and be able to tolerate in the Netherlands.

From 2002 to 2012, immigration and Islam topped the national political agenda. Instead of on ethnocentric grounds or out of fear for competition with Christianity, attacks on Islam have been cloaked as a defence of secularist and liberal values, to a certain extent reopening old wounds between secularists and (Christian) religious conservative minorities in the Netherlands as well. The paradox remains that liberal and tolerant traditions have been used not to include minorities, but to exclude them. That paradox has raised difficult, confusing questions about the actual meaning of tolerance and liberal principles in the Netherlands.[29] Does liberalism itself privilege a certain culture?[30] Do solidarity

---

[27]Penninx, "Dutch Immigrant Policies", 241–54.
[28]Law on Civic Education Abroad, 1 January 2007.
[29]Duyvendak, *Een eensgezinde, vooruitstrevende natie*.
[30]Zizek, "Tolerance as an Ideological Category".

and the redistribution of welfare apply to newcomers? Does a liberal *choice* to live a pious life as a Muslim, thereby rejecting the Western capitalist culture in which autonomy and individual freedoms stand higher than collective solidarity, connection and the responsibility for the family, make one a security threat? Does liberalism need to defend itself?

To illustrate how the debates on Dutch identity and Islam are intertwined, one can quote some of the statements made during a plenary Senate debate on a bill to ban ritual, unstunned, slaughtering. The MP presenting this bill, member of the Party of the Animals, perhaps the most recent expression of the changing political landscape, sees enhancing animal welfare as a form of societal progress:

> Reviewing and reforming old traditions is a logical element of societal development. (...) This has held true for thinking regarding women's rights, the rights of homosexuals, freedom to chose a marital partner and many other issues that can touch partly on religious beliefs.[31]

Many relatively new parties tended to support this reasoning, placing 'progressive' values hierarchically above religious freedoms. For example, the left-leaning Green Party (*GroenLinks*) stated:

> Freedom of religion is not an absolute constitutional right. It is written in the Constitution that exceptions can be made to this freedom and the European Convention for Human Rights as well stipulates that freedom of religion can be curbed when judged necessary to guarantee public order, health or decency to protect the rights and freedoms of others.[32]

The rightwing Freedom Party (PVV) argued:

> The question is whether we want this type of slaughtering practices in a civilised country like the Netherlands. (...) It cannot be that groups, on the basis of their religion or ideology, demand an exception to the law. There are countries where on the basis of a religion or an ideology people are stoned to death and are being hanged. Women also are suppressed because of religious prescriptions.[33]

Instead, the more traditional parties tended to evoke the traditional 'Dutch mentality'. The Labour Party, gaining approval from the Christian Democrats, reasoned:

> Respect for constitutional rights, including the freedom of religion and minority rights, is one of the tenets that have characterised the Netherlands for centuries, as a country of tolerance and pluralism.[34]

---

[31]Minutes of the Dutch Parliament, I, 2011–2012, 31571, nr. 12, 18.
[32]Minutes of the Dutch Parliament, I, 2011–2012, 31571, nr. 12, 9.
[33]Minutes of the Dutch Parliament, I, 2011–2012, 31571, nr. 12, 26.
[34]Minutes of the Dutch Parliament, I, 2011–2012, 31571, nr. 12, 2.

The conservative Christian parties showed the greatest indignation, uttering:

> This bill is part of a secularized societal field, in which the freedom of religion in the public space is increasingly under pressure.[35]

And:

> The Netherlands has always been a country welcoming religious minorities. Here, they could experience and practice their religion in freedom. The majority knew that they had to respect minorities and minorities amongst each other gave each other space. That was what made the Netherlands a culturally strong place. We have always been proud of that tolerance. Banning the ritual form of slaughter puts great tension on the freedom of religion. In the eyes of these minorities, this terminates the special Dutch cultural agreement of tolerance of minorities and religiosity experience.[36]

The most conservative of all (SGP), summed up the views of the new political actors with the words:

> Many seem to be able to empathize better with the existence of a chicken than with that of a religious person.[37]

Conclusion

The Islam debate in Dutch politics focuses on the impact 'Islamic values' would have on the liberal, progressive and relatively secular image of Dutch society. The Dutch debate is not only *about* Islam, but also *uses* Islam as a proxy for other questions of national identity. Attacks on Islam have been cloaked as a defence of long-cherished liberal achievements. A conflict has emerged between those judging society fundamentally tolerant and inclusive for religious minorities and those that identify with the progressive, secularist values that have increasingly dominated the country since the crumbling of traditional pillarised communities. By articulating views on Islam, the traditional and newly established parties have provoked each other into questioning their respective fundamental beliefs and values. For some, Islam is the antithesis of Dutch tolerance, for others that tolerance is the cause of the problems in the first place, and for still others the real issue at stake is that the Dutch have forgotten how to be tolerant. With the Muslim population growing steadily, the question whether Islam is compatible with Dutch values can attract the entire range of answers: from an explicit yes to an explicit no. Most likely, for every position, a certain practice of Islam can be found to confirm as well as to reject that view.

---

[35]Minutes of the Dutch Parliament, I, 2011–2012, 31571, nr. 12, 29.
[36]Minutes of the Dutch Parliament, I, 2011–2012, 31571, nr. 12, 30.
[37]Minutes of the Dutch Parliament, I, 2011–2012, 31571, nr. 12, 11.

References

Anderson, B. *Imagined Communities: Reflections on the Origins and Spread of Nationalism*. London: Verso, 1991.

Beune, H. and J.A. Hessels. *Minderheid – Minder recht?* The Hague: Staatsuitgeverij, 1983.

Bijsterveld, S.C. van "The Legal Status of Islam in the Kingdom of the Netherlands". In *Islam and European Legal Systems*, edited by S. Ferrari and A. Bradney. Dartmouth: Ashgate, 2000.

Bohemen, S. van., R. Kemmers and W. de Koster. "Seculiere intolerantie: morele progressiviteit en afwijzing van de Islam in Nederland". *Sociologie* 8, no. 2 (2012): 199–218.

Duyvendak, J. *Een eensgezinde, vooruitstrevende natie: Over de mythe van "de" individualisering en de toekomst van de sociologie*. Amsterdam: Vossiuspress, 2004.

Fortuyn, P. *De puinhopen van acht jaar Paars*. Uithoorn: Karakters Uitgevers, 2002.

Gellner, E. *Nations and Nationalism*. Oxford: Basil Blackwell, 1983.

Hendriks, F. "Contextualizing the Dutch Drop in Political Trust: Connecting Underlying Factors". *International Review of Administrative Sciences* 75, no. 3 (2009): 473–91.

Lijphart, A. *The Politics of Accommodation*. Berkeley: University of California Press, 1975.

Noort, W. J. van. *Nederland als voorbeeldige natie*. Hilversum: Uitgeverij Verloren, 2006.

Pelikaan, H.S., L. de Lange and T. van der Meer. "Fortuyn's Legacy: Party System Change in the Netherlands". *Comparative European Politics* 5, no. 3 (2007): 282–302.

Penninx, R. "Dutch Immigrant Policies Before and After the Van Gogh Murder". *Journal of International Migration and Integration* 7, no. 2 (2006): 241–54.

Rath, J., A. Meyer and T. Sunier. "The Establishment of Islamic Institutions in a De-pillarizing Society". *Tijdschrift voor Economische en Sociale Geografie* 88, no. 4 (1997): 389–95.

Schmeets, H. and R. van der Bie. "Religie aan het begin van de 21ste eeuw". In *CBS Rapport 2009*. The Hague: Centraal Bureau voor de Statistiek, 2009. http://www.cbs.nl/NR/rdonlyres/953535E3-9D25-4C28-A70D-7A4AEEA76E27/0/2008e16pubpdf.

Sengers, E. and T. Sunier, eds. *Religious Newcomers and the Nation-state*. Delft: Eburon Uitgeverij, 2010.

Slauerhoff, J. J. "In Nederland". In *Verzamelde gedichten Deel 2*, J. J. Slauerhoff. Den Haag: A.A.M. Stols, (tweede druk) 1947.

Sunier, T. "Islam in the Netherlands: a Nation Despite Religious Communities?" In *Religious Newcomers and the Nation-state*, edited by E. Sengers and T. Sunier. Delft: Eburon Uitgeverij, 2010.

Vink, M. P. "Dutch 'Multiculturalism' beyond the Pillarisation Myth". *Political Studies Review* 5, no. 3 (2007): 337–50.

Wetenschappelijke Raad voor het Regeringsbeleid (WRR). *Ethnische Minderheden*, Rapporten aan de Regering 17. The Hague: Staatsuitgeverij, 1979.

Zizek, S. "Tolerance as an Ideological Category". *Critical Inquiry* 34, no. 4 (Summer 2008): 660–82.

Islam and Muslim Communities in the UK: Multiculturalism, Faith and Security

Catherine Fieschi and Nick Johnson

This piece examines the relationship of Muslim communities to the UK mainstream between 2005 and 2010. Using the dual backdrop of the country's embedded multiculturalism policy and its counter-terrorism strategy implemented through the Prevent agenda, the authors brush a picture of a tense yet ultimately resilient relationship. While Prevent was often accused of leading to a securitisation of community policy, it is arguable that tensions have led to increased visibility and leadership capacity from the Muslim community, and a recognition of their role and diversity on behalf of the public and the government.

The focus of this article is on the relationship between Muslim communities and the mainstream in the UK as they were shaped and perceived throughout a specific, and particularly significant period, from the immediate aftermath of the July 2005 attacks in London to the worsening of the economic crisis and the change of government in 2010. This period is worth examining for two reasons.

The first reason is that it captures the state of the relationship at the time of the attacks of 2005, shaped as it was by several decades of multicultural policy, but also lacking as a result of the nature of this particular version of multiculturalism.

The second reason is that this period marks a significant turning point in the relationship between Muslim communities and the mainstream: a worsening followed by improvement. The worsening is in great part due to the main tension at work throughout the period in question: one that pits a security agenda (and discourse) against a cohesion agenda (and accompanying discourse) – the latter being the 1990s incarnation of the British multicultural project. The result is the perception (by Muslim communities and their leaders) of, at best, confusion, at worst, manipulation. For non-Muslims, the tension was experienced as a set of mixed messages that soured community relations and undermined trust in the security forces and police, as well as community leaders.

However riven and tense the relationship has been, seven years after the 2005 attacks, over a decade after the 2001 attacks in the United States and the Bradford riots, it would seem that the multicultural framework has prevailed over the forces of deterioration and conflict: Muslim communities have come out of the period better organised, better represented, better understood and, dare we say it, better integrated into the polity. The aim of this article is to show how such an outcome was snatched from the teeth of chaos over the course of a very specific period.

Some might argue that the sharpness of the recession has refocused attention away from such matters, whilst others might argue, quite rightly, that the existence of groups such as the English Defence League (EDL) put pay to any notion of improving relationships. But recessions can make matters worse in terms of community and race relations, and this hasn't been the case in the context of the UK. As for the EDL, while it is a deeply problematic group that has the capacity to make life very difficult in a number of areas, they do not reflect mainstream opinion, nor have they been able to mobilise it.

The British context

Two important contextual issues need to be borne in mind when discussing the changing role of Islam in the UK: the first is a heated debate about Britain's multicultural framework of policies with particular introspection on the left of the political spectrum. Thus the growth in Islam's importance needs to be understood as part of this ongoing discussion about diversity in 21st century Britain. The second is that it is not only Islam's place that has grown in UK public life, but that of religion in general (recent 2011 census figures suggest that citizens of Christian background are increasingly secular, but that this is not the case for Muslims).

A beleaguered multicultural framework

Partly fuelled by the US civil rights movement and the increasingly vocal claims of ethnic minority communities, Britain awoke to what was then termed "a race relations problem" during the 1960s. Perceptions of growing immigrant numbers against a backdrop of turbulent industrial relations and rising unemployment gave rise to speeches such as Enoch Powell's well-known – and often misquoted – "Rivers of blood" in 1968. This rapidly led to the development of some new radical ideas in relation to the management of diversity. In Canada and the United States, this debate was particularly rich and ideas of multiculturalism began to emerge as a form of political management. Yet as pointed out by Tahir Abbas, quoting Bhikhu Parekh, multiculturalism is "best understood neither as a political doctrine nor a philosophical school with a distinct theory but as a perspective on or a way of viewing human life".[1]

Multiculturalism is best explained as resting on four central insights: The first, is that human beings are culturally embedded – in the sense that they grow up and live within a culturally structured world and organise their lives and social relations in terms of a culturally derived system of meaning and significance. Second, that different cultures represent different systems of meaning and visions of life. And, third, that every culture is internally plural and reflects a continuing conversation between its different traditions and strands of thought.[2]

The fourth and crucial insight is provided by the Canadian philosopher Charles Taylor, whose own understanding of multiculturalism is shaped by his communitarian views on the one hand and his experience of a Québecois society embedded within the Canadian multicultural project on the other. Taylor's perspective is critical because it lays out the principles of what has become known as the "politics of recognition" upon which any form of multicultural policy framework rests. The central premise is that different groups need to give allegiance to the same institutions. To do that, they have to feel a sense of identification with and belonging to the wider institutional framework. In turn, that relies on confidence in the group that the prevailing institutions will understand, accommodate and reflect their interests. Such interests are bound up in identities which depend heavily on characteristics like race, ethnicity and – added later – religion. It is important, therefore, for minorities to see an accurate reflection of their sense of self along these different dimensions in the public sphere and that these identities (or identification markers) be acknowledged by other groups in society as well.

For the UK, the kind of multiculturalism adopted from the 1970s onwards was a way of reconciling a certain pragmatism about living together – in practice rather than in theory – with a striking traditional belief in the role of community, neighbourhood initiatives, cooperatives (in a word: the vibrant civil society that provided the societal glue required to live together in a land of unwritten, or at least uncodified, rules). This multiculturalism was, therefore, never enshrined as a doctrine, let alone the national ideology that it is in Canada, but rather as a set of principles that encouraged the celebration of diversity, dialogue between cultures and a measure of minority protection that built on the various versions of the Race Relations Act (1965, 1968, 1976, 2000) and the British Nationality Act of 1948 (and 1981).

---

[1] Parekh, *Rethinking Multiculturalism.*

[2] Parekh discusses how the early 1970s marked the emergence of the multicultural movement at first in Canada and Australia and then in the US, UK, Germany and elsewhere. What Parekh calls the "multiculturalist perspective" is composed of the interplay of these three important and complementary insights (Parekh, *Rethinking Multiculturalism*).

Significantly however, it moved the UK toward a vision of society based on distinct group identities defined along ethnic or racial lines and this principle came to underpin multiculturalist policies, especially those advanced by the state at both national and local level. The result was a framework of policies that encouraged the affirmation of such identities as the basis of political and social organisation as well as the creation of community networks and programmes based on ethnic or racial affiliation – thereby lending legitimacy to Taylor's view that recognition of identity by others is important for a sense of well-being.

Multiculturalism also increasingly became seen by both the media and the public as a vehicle of the political left, with ethnic minorities increasingly favouring the Labour Party. Whilst many mainstream Conservatives had disavowed Powell's rhetoric in 1968, behind the scenes many were sympathetic. Certainly, the right became the voice of those who wanted to limit immigration. The left's response was an ever more aggressive assertion of multiculturalism. Labour administrations in town halls across the country diverted more resources to minority communities, and encouraged greater organisation and representation amongst ethnic groups. This bore political fruit with the election of the first ethnic minority MPs to parliament in 1987, all of them representing Labour.

Multiculturalism increasingly came under attack from the right, which complained that it gave special treatment to minority communities. It came to be grouped together with such issues as "health and safety" and was mocked for being nothing more than "political correctness" without any substance. It remained, however, part of left political orthodoxy until the start of this century, a period that culminated in the report of the *Commission on a Multi-ethnic Britain*, published in 2000.[3] This once again reasserted the importance of a multicultural framework for race relations, based as it was on the idea that one's polity required people to be organised as a community of communities and not just as a community of individuals.

Simultaneously, however, a number of events began to cast doubt over the benefits of multiculturalism in Britain. Firstly, the brutal and racially motivated murder of the teenager Stephen Lawrence in 1993 and the botched police investigation of his killers raised significant questions about how much Britain's attitudes to minority communities had really changed and, therefore, what kind of claims to success multiculturalist policies could make. An inquiry into the case, led by Sir William MacPherson, was launched by the incoming Labour government in 1997 and its final publication in 1999 was a damning indictment of the Metropolitan Police, which was found to be profoundly institutionally racist. This was followed just two years later by riots in several northern towns in 2001. Prompted by clashes between Asian teenagers and the resurgent far right

---

[3] Runnymede, *Parekh Report*, 11 October 2000, http://www.runnymedetrust.org/reportIntroduction.html.

in the shape of the British National Party (BNP), the disturbances exposed fault-lines within Britain's communities. The subsequent government report highlighted "the depth of polarisation in our towns and cities. This means that many communities operate on the basis of a series of parallel lives."[4]

Thus began a debate on segregation and fragmentation that was already well underway before the collapse of the twin towers in 2001, and certainly before the 7/7 attacks in 2005 – in other words, long before the focus fell upon Britain's Muslim communities. The government's new phrase of choice was "community cohesion" which went through a number of reinterpretations over the years but essentially shifted the focus from promoting group identity to promoting interaction between groups. This debate broke out into the open in 2004 with two high profile interventions, ostensibly from the liberal left, that tried to call time upon Britain's multiculturalism. First came an assault from the editor of *Prospect* magazine, David Goodhart, who argued that there was an inherent tension between solidarity – high social cohesion and generous welfare paid out of a progressive tax system – and diversity – equal respect for a wide range of peoples, values and ways of life.[5] This was followed by an attack on the divisiveness of multiculturalism by Trevor Phillips, then chair of the Commission for Racial Equality (CRE). The following year, Phillips would famously claim that Britain was "sleepwalking to segregation".[6] However, by then the bombings on the London underground had occurred and the nature of the debate had entirely changed.

The balance sheet

Overall, we can claim a positive balance sheet for multiculturalism in its time. Over the years since the 1960s, Britain has undoubtedly seen a reduction in racism and intolerance and a greater appreciation of diversity. However, inequality has remained stubbornly ingrained within some ethnic minority communities. In its valedictory publication in 2007, the CRE pointed out that an ethnic minority British baby born today is sadly still more likely to go on to receive poor quality education, be paid less, live in substandard housing, be in poor health and be discriminated against in other ways than his or her white contemporaries.

By the start of this century therefore, multiculturalism was coming under increased attack and was no longer the default language of the left. A critique emerged which argued that, despite it obvious successes in the past, multiculturalism had had its day. At its core, the argument was that we had focussed too much

---

[4] Cantle, *Community Cohesion*, http://resources.cohesioninstitute.org.uk/Publications/Documents/Document/DownloadDocumentsFile.aspx?recordId=96&file=PDFversion.
[5] D. Goodhart, "The Discomfort of Strangers", *The Guardian*, 24 February 2004, http://www.guardian.co.uk/politics/2004/feb/24/race.eu.
[6] Phillips, "After 7/7 Sleepwalking to Segregation".

upon culture at the expense of socio-economic indicators and improvements in life-chances.

Some even claim that our "increased understanding" of Islam is no more than an "Orientalism take II", a general Western *mea culpa* which is just as reifying of Islam as a culture and as a faith as our previous less reverent take on it. Exotic fascination has been replaced with patronising reverence at best, fearful certainty at worst. For example while we no longer look upon the veil as expressing a fundamental Oriental otherness, we have reified it as a quaint cultural expression or fetishised it as a symbol of Islam's fundamental backwardness, neither of which captures the diversity or subtlety of reality. It is in this context as much as any debate about terrorism that we need to look at Britain's current relationship to Islam.

The prime minister that "did God"

Faith was never a comfortable part of Britain's multicultural settlement: our notions of diversity were about race and ethnicity. In part because the Church of England often provided a point of integration and connection between host and new communities. In part though, it had to do with a British rejection of faith in the public sphere (a paradox of course given the lack of formal separation between church and state). This was a notion particularly championed by the left which remained sceptical of the power of religion and, indeed, associated the Church of England with a conservative view of society which did not equate with the vibrant diversity of Britain as it approached the millennium. This anachronistic vision was seemingly best encapsulated by former Prime Minister John Major's expression of British identity as nuns riding to evensong past the village cricket pitch.

This aversion to faith was challenged in the first instance not by Islam but by the overt religiosity of Tony Blair, who made his faith central not just to his personal character but to his political philosophy. The story of the struggle between Blair and his advisors over the place of religion in public life is a well documented tale. And one in which even the most gifted spin doctor is eventually flattened by Blair's convictions. The incident of the *Vanity Fair* interview (in 2003) for instance, during which a touchy Alastair Campbell interrupted his boss to abruptly interject that "we don't do God",[7] went down at the time as an extraordinary illustration of the power of unelected officials in Blair's entourage, but nearly a decade hence, it feels like an anachronism. Since then, both as PM and certainly since his stepping down, religion has been at the forefront of Blair's public life. Blair has since converted to Catholicism and founded the Tony Blair Faith Foundation for inter-faith dialogue.

---

[7] C. Brown, "Campbell Interrupted Blair as he Spoke of his Faith: 'We don't do God'", *The Telegraph*, 4 May 2003, http://www.telegraph.co.uk/news/uknews/1429109/Campbell-interrupted-Blair-as-he-spoke-of-his-faith-We-dont-do-God.html.

The impact of Blair's attitude (and his wife's) toward religion and spirituality in general (including the presence in a Labour government of overtly conservative Catholic ministers such as Ruth Kelly) is not to be underestimated: religion went from being the preserve of conservative (small "c") classes and derided by progressives (despite a strong Christian Socialist strand in the Labour Party) to being once again an acceptable topic of debate even on the left, cohabiting, more or less happily, with the tolerant liberalism instilled by multiculturalism.[8]

Religion's renewed presence in public discourse could lead to the impression that the numbers have increased, yet this is not the case. Aside from a numerical increase in those who label themselves of a Muslim faith, the numbers show no increase in church attendance or denominational affiliation. According to the Office for National Statistics and the 2001 census, there were 41 million Christians in the UK in 2001, making up 72 percent of the population. Though how much this is actually a reflection of religiosity as opposed to an easy label adopted by people for whom religion plays little or no role in their life is difficult to say. People with no religion formed the second largest group, comprising 15 percent of the population.

About one in 20 (5 percent) of the population belonged to a non-Christian religious denomination of which Muslims were the largest group. There were 1.6 million Muslims living in Britain in 2001. This group comprised 3 percent of the total population and over half (52 percent) of the non-Christian religious population. Church attendance continues to fall, though of those who attend the proportion of 16 to 25 year olds is slightly on the increase. As for mosque attendance, while still very low for young Muslims, it seems to be on the increase.[9]

Numbers aside, faith has itself once again become a subject for policy. There is a national Interfaith Network, comprising many local organisations aimed at

---

[8] In mid-September 2010, it was interesting to note both the negative press around the Pope's visit to the UK (which included a letter denouncing his presence signed by a number of prominent British figures), as well as the furore around Baroness Warsi's (Co-Chairman of the Conservative Party) comments in Oxford at the Conference of Church of England Bishops that this coalition government "does God", http://www.guardian.co.uk/politics/2010/sep/15/coalition-does-god-baroness-warsi.

[9] Ascertaining what might be exact numbers is extremely difficult. A lack of information is only one of the hurdles. The other is the manipulation and "contextualisation" of the figures. While most organisations involved in monitoring (both Muslim and non-Muslim) can claim fairly confidently that there has been an increase in mosque attendance, especially by young Muslims, this is often couched in terms that do not allow for even a guess as to what those numbers might be. Christian Research (http://www.christian-research.org/ Christian Research) revealed relative trends in 2008, that put at 683,000 the number of Muslims attending mosque. But in 2004, *Christianity Today* (http://www.christiantoday.co.uk/) had placed that number at 930,000, thereby claiming that Christians had been overtaken by Muslims in terms of religious observance. The difficulty lies in part in such studies measuring "attendance" along once-a-week Christian lines, whereas mosque attendance and being a part of the mosque community – especially for youth – can take many other forms. It is however predicted with some confidence that given the demographics in most Muslim communities and the tendency of mosques to recruit youth, the number for 2013 will be greater than 2001.

bringing the faiths together. Religion and belief were introduced as a "protected characteristic" under Britain's extensive anti-discrimination legislation and the government has even gone so far as to introduce a national Interfaith strategy and set up a "faith unit" within Whitehall's permanent structures. Indeed, in recent years, faith has become more dominant in political debate than race. The future of many of these initiatives is now more uncertain through a combination of the severe public spending cuts and the new British government's indifference to much of this agenda. Rather than promising a massive ideological reversion, the likelihood is that the cohesion agenda will drift into disrepair, but that faith will remain a topic for debate without enough reference to the communities into which it is embedded.

It is clear that the combination of the role of religion in Britain as well as the multicultural framework within which social and economic choices were being made led to a situation in which religions and other groups had much to gain by organising, but paradoxically, one which left them vulnerable to targeting should one community in particular be associated with a problem. When 9/11 happened, and then subsequently even more so in the wake of 7/7, the Muslim community (in the singular at the time) and the multicultural framework were left open to criticism as well as instrumentalisation.

Multiculturalism and UK Muslims

It is important to evaluate the position of the Muslim community in the UK in September 2001. To some extent it is worth pointing out that while multiculturalism had indeed made an impact on Muslims in the UK, Islam and the Muslim communities had not initially been the targets or principal concerns of those who advocated multiculturalism. Britain's postwar race relations were fixed for a number of years by the arrival of the Windrush generation of Afro-Caribbeans in the late 1940s and their subsequent history of discrimination and protest. That protest frequently turned violent, particularly in clashes with the police – from Notting Hill in 1958, through Brixton in 1981 to the Broadwater Farm estate in 1985. Indeed, the criminal justice field was central to debates over racial equality with the Scarman Report after the Brixton riots becoming the basis for a set of police reforms that to this day inform the notion of community policing and much of the discussion and practice that have animated the UK since 7/7. As we shall see, despite the context being very different, the experiences of Muslims after 7/7 bear some resemblance to those of the Afro-Caribbean community.

In many respects the Muslim communities were not as far along in their multicultural response as others were. In part because they were more isolated, but also because religion was a late addition to the list of collective identities. Statistics of racial inequality were just that – about race. Religion was not even asked about in the Census until 2001.[10]

Muslim political representation was also not as robust as that for other minority communities. The main organisation that had emerged as the voice of the Muslim community was the Muslim Council of Britain (MCB). The story of the emergence and role of the MCB is a complex one, but most simply told by the political journalist Martin Bright:

> The origins of the MCB can be traced to the *Satanic Verses* affair, when Iqbal Sacranie came to prominence as a leader of the opposition to Salman Rushdie's novel. The idea for an umbrella organisation for British Islam was first floated when Michael Howard was Home Secretary in the last Conservative Government. But the idea was taken up with particular alacrity by Jack Straw, always with an eye to his Muslim constituents in Blackburn, and the organisation was officially founded in November 1997. Straw championed its cause, first as Home Secretary and then, after the 2001 election, as Foreign Secretary.[11]

The report by Bright, from which this quote is drawn, was controversial and fuelled the debate concerning which groups governments should (and could) be seen to legitimately engage with for security and other purposes. But more to the point here, the report highlighted what 7/7 had laid bare: that despite an active policy of multiculturalism, the government had only *one, single* interlocutor when it came to the Muslim community (still very much perceived in the singular at the time) – and not a terribly reputable one at that. In the wake of 7/7 it became glaringly apparent to both the UK public, and even more so to the government, that Muslim communities were much more diverse than this umbrella organisation had led them to believe, that many did not feel in the slightest represented by it, and more importantly that many felt let down by the government's single-minded pursuit of the relationship with the MCB, which they did not respect and which many did not trust.

This is an important point, because it means that in some respects the Muslim communities had only benefited from a variant of multiculturalism which is more akin to patronage networks than to representation and access. What is meant is that in pursuing a single relationship with the MCB, the web of organisations and variety of leaders that multiculturalism is meant to create never had the chance to flourish. As such, the multicultural framework did not – could not – deliver for the Muslim communities because it was stunted.

This duality – a multicultural system capable of much, but that had not delivered for this particular community – is important because it means that 7/7 marked

---

[10] Thus, for most ethnic minority communities, their housing conditions, their educational attainment and their general health are likely to be worse than the national average. This can be broken down into 'Asian', but it is not as easy to do for Muslim communities.

[11] Bright, *When Progressives Treat with Reactionaries*, 12.

the realisation both that the multiculturalism agenda needed to be stepped up in Muslim communities and that it was useful for security purposes – paradoxically, at the very time at which its relevance and utility were more generally being called into question for the UK as a whole. While complex, this course of action makes perfect sense in the context of the Muslim communities – multiculturalism was deemed useful to bolster fragmented relationships within the communities. But "community cohesion" was perceived as the policy *du jour* at a national level to foster relationships between communities. A set of security concerns were then grafted onto this dual-track system.

The Prevent strategy and the securitisation of state services

The next sections of the article are a good illustration of the weight of events on existing policymaking.

Despite the re-evaluation of multiculturalism, and despite its weaknesses (outlined earlier), where multiculturalism had been effectively implemented prior to 7/7, the Prevent agenda put in place in the wake of 7/7 was perceived both as effective and as legitimate by communities. Where multiculturalism was stunted, Prevent policies were perceived as nothing more than the victimisation of Muslims, the securitisation of public services and the annexation of the cohesion agenda for counter-terrorism purposes. But in both cases, the concomitant implementation of these two, potentially contradictory agendas (especially when it was done from within the same government department, as was the case with the newly created Department for Communities and Local Government), gave rise to confusion and scepticism.

Multiculturalism after 7/7

As discussed earlier, multiculturalism was already under sustained assault from the right and increasing questioning from the left when it began to be appreciated through the prism of terrorism. In December 2002, a group comprising the Home Office, the Local Government Association, the Commission for Racial Equality and the Inter Faith Network published definitive guidance on community cohesion which claimed that:

- Communities should show a common vision and a sense of belonging;
- Diversity of different backgrounds and circumstances are appreciated and positively valued;
- Those from different backgrounds have similar life opportunities;
- There are strong and positive relationships between people from different backgrounds in the workplace, in schools and within neighbourhoods.

With some changes at the margins, notably by the Commission for Integration and Cohesion in 2007 and by the government the following year, this has remained the main statement of intent for government policy in the past decade and multi-culturalism was for all intents and purposes replaced by Community Cohesion.[12]

Relations with minority communities were already being reconsidered when terrorism struck. And while 9/11 had some impact upon UK public opinion, it was not until the reality of British-born, relatively "well integrated" bombers attacking the London underground struck home, that security became a driving force in policymaking and the lens through which community relations would be assessed and conducted.

The first reaction immediately post 7/7 was largely one of panic. The prime minister announced a Commission on Integration at a live press conference, much to the surprise of his civil servants who then scrambled to work out what this would mean in practice. For Blair, significantly given his own religiosity, this was a commission looking at the role of faith, and inter-faith work in Britain. However, he faced a battle with his then Home Secretary, Charles Clarke, who was reluctant to give the commission such a focus. This led to delays and resulted in a far more locally-focussed inquiry into how communities could interact with one another.

A more immediate reaction than the Commission, was the creation in summer 2005 of a series of task groups looking at the role of Muslims in the UK and what could be done to increase resilience against violent extremism. The task forces and the utter (if well meaning) incompetence that characterised them were revealing of a government that did not know its Muslim population or even have a passing acquaintance with mainstream tenets of Islam – and that had relied naively on a small number of individuals who had led them, at best, down political blind alleys, at worst, into dangerous positions.[13]

Though there was little evidence of a strategic approach, it was clear that from then on, cohesion policy, certainly at a governmental level, would be driven by a preoccupation with the Muslim communities and the threat of terrorism.

---

[12] This has not been without its critics, traditionally from the left and anti-racist campaigners who feel that it does not do enough to tackle discrimination and puts too much of an onus upon minority communities rather than the white majority to achieve cohesion. A chief proponent of community cohesion has been Ted Cantle, who led one of the government's investigations into the northern riots of 2001. Much of his approach is rooted in contact theory which became increasingly recognised as a tool in Northern Ireland (Crisp and Hewstone, *Multiple Social Categorization*). For Cantle, strong and positive relationships between communities need to build on the basis of shared experiences and meaningful interaction (Cantle, *Community Cohesion*, 29). Cantle's critics though argue that his ideas are rooted in a more assimilationist approach and ignore structural inequalities (Wetherell, *Identity, Ethnic Diversity and Community Cohesion*).

[13] On this, see the report by Bright, *When Progressives Treat with Reactionaries*. For post 7/7 remarks and accounts, see especially chapter 3 and the remarks by Lady Falkner (member of the Working Group on Tackling Extremism and Radicalisation), as well comments by Khurshid Ahmed of the British Muslim Forum, 27-8.

Despite the prevailing critique of multiculturalism that took it to task for slotting people into distinct community identities, the government's response to terrorism was to default to this approach when it came to the Muslim community.

The paradox in the case of Muslim communities is double. First, the Muslim communities started benefitting from some of the basic tenets of multicultural policies (in terms of leadership development, support and recognition) just as the policy was being wound down for everyone else. This led to the second part, which was a shift toward a deeper multiculturalism that encompassed a move away from interfaith while focusing on the Muslim communities more exclusively.

Prevent in practice

To respond to the threat of international terrorism, the British government established a counter-terrorism strategy known as Contest. 'Prevent' was one of the 4 'P's of this strategy and it was designed to stop people becoming terrorists or supporting violent extremists. The other 'P's were

Pursue – to stop terrorist attacks;
Prepare – where an attack cannot be stopped, to mitigate its impact;
Protect – to strengthen overall protection against terrorist attacks.

In a nutshell, Prevent was an attempt to "communitise" security through a system of cross-departmental partnerships and the delivery of programmes through local authorities in partnership with local and community associations. The agenda brought together the Department of Children, Schools and Families, the Department for Communities and Local Government (created out of the Home Office in 2005), the Department of Justice, the Home Office, the Department for Universities and Skills and, finally, the Department for Culture, Media and Sports. The Prevent strategy had five strands aimed at addressing the main factors identified as the key drivers of radicalisation in UK communities:

- challenging the violent extremist ideology and supporting mainstream voices;
- disrupting those who promote violent extremism and supporting the institutions where they are active;
- supporting individuals who are being targeted for recruitment to the cause of violent extremism;
- increasing the resilience of communities to violent extremism;
- addressing the grievances that ideologues are exploiting.

In practice, the Prevent agenda was designed to create a dense web of agreements and partnerships between community groups and programmes working hand in hand with local communities. Any program that was seen as building such ties between the local authority (including the police), local government services and community associations could qualify for Prevent funding.

Prevent can be seen as a logical development: the result of a public services reform agenda that privileged users and local delivery on the one hand, and community based policing on the other. Prevent was a consistent link in this chain – it joined up government, it was partnership-led and used public services as a means to transform both local communities and affect the national landscape. In other words, though it was controversial, Prevent was consistent with government policies that pre-dated the terrorist attacks of 2005. And, in comparison to the state-led, top-down policy and the brazen incursions of security forces into every aspect of public life that characterised many other European reactions (for e.g. the Netherlands), the UK's attempt to diversify its approach to security by tasking public services to help deliver it, as opposed to tasking security agencies with invading vaster swathes of the public sphere, was quite pioneering. If ultimately problematic.

Put in place effectively in late 2008, the Prevent agenda was a hugely controversial topic in the UK, so much so that in 2010, the fledgling programme had its first official review. This was followed by its virtual termination by David Cameron's coalition government, which repatriated *all* of the Prevent responsibilities to the Home Office, thereby fundamentally altering the very nature of the agenda and its community and public service objectives. Derided by some Muslim associations as the "provoke" agenda, ridiculed by others for its ineptness, grudgingly appreciated – or simply exploited by those who benefited from its largesse (45 million pounds over a couple of years), the Prevent agenda came under fire from many quarters. For example, writing in *The Guardian* in September 2009, Yahya Birt (a prominent Muslim scholar and commentator and former director of the influential Muslim organisation, The City Circle) gave voice to sentiments that were widely shared across Muslim communities in the UK:

> Under the Prevent policy, aimed at countering violent extremism, local authorities have had to prioritise counter-terrorism. Youth services, community safety and neighbourhood teams, social inclusion and regeneration teams are all being inveigled into this cause. Community workers are concerned about how to preserve relationships of trust with those they are helping, particularly with Muslim young people. One youth worker I spoke to complained of police intrusion into his work, of being pressurised to reveal details about his clients and to breach his professional code of confidentiality. Youth services, he said, were being driven towards counter-terrorism and away from drugs and criminality.[14]

Inayat Bunglawala of the MCB writing at roughly the same time, had this to say on the shortcomings of Prevent:

> Yesterday the *Guardian* reported that John Denham, the new secretary of state at the Communities and Local Government Department, wants to see a policy shift away

---

[14] Y. Birt, "Don't Repeat this Mistake", *The Guardian*, 14 September 2009, http://www.guardian.co.uk/commentisfree/belief/2009/sep/14/islam-extremism-far-right-terrorism.

from defining the government's relationship with Muslim communities solely in terms of tackling extremism while also developing a more explicit strategy to resist white racist extremism. This should be applauded by all who desire to live in safer communities.[15]

The final paragraph sums up the feelings of many both within and outside of the Muslim community: that Prevent had used the knowledge gained from years of multiculturalism (however stunted) in order to categorize communities, use this knowledge against them, securitise the relationship and had essentially asked them to spy on each other in return for grants.[16]

In essence, Prevent was widely perceived as intelligence gathering under the guise of community cohesion. Furthermore, criticisms abounded as to its effectiveness. Yahya Birt, again:

> The vast majority of Muslim institutions that have signed up to Prevent are too distant from the violent fringe – their response has always been to kick the al-Muhajirouns of this world out of the mosques. They have felt more comfortable using Prevent funds for pet projects that have little direct impact: a government-commissioned audit found that only 3 percent of projects targeted those "glorifying or justifying violent extremism". Why would this blanket approach work any better in preventing far-right terrorism? We need universal reasons – not counter-terrorist ones – to tackle inequality on a basis that all British citizens can accept as equitable and fair.[17]

The main debate around Islam in the UK in the past few years has been dominated by Prevent and the fallout from Prevent. Prevent has drawn messy but effective battle lines: between those who argue that combating extremism is a job for professional counter-terrorists and those who feel that this needs to be part of a community agenda; as well as between those who argue that combating Islamic extremism is about countering a "perverted" theological narrative with an "accurate" theological counter-narrative against those for whom it is a social matter of community cohesion, rather than a matter of theological accuracy.

Prevent was to be this broader, more inclusive strategy but relying on a multicultural revival for the Muslim communities and then co-opting many of the cohesion mechanisms for security purposes, it may have neither served its purpose nor made the Muslim communities more receptive to the government's appeal for help and self-regulation.

---

[15] I. Bunglawala, *The Guardian*, "Calling Time on Prevent", 14 August 2009.

[16] Reading the transcript of the House of Commons Communities and Local Government Preventing Violent Extremism Committee debate and comments gives a very good overview of the criticism and concerns of a vast number of UK actors regarding the Prevent agenda, http://www.publications.parliament.uk/pa/cm200910/cmselect/cmcomloc/65/65.pdf.

[17] Y. Birt, "Don't Repeat this Mistake", *The Guardian*, 14 September 2009.

As pointed out by the Local Government Association and by many others, both in the UK and elsewhere:

> There are subtle differences between work intended to improve community cohesion and work specifically targeted at Prevent. Community cohesion projects are about building stronger relationships between people of different backgrounds. Prevent is about continuing and enhancing the work that local authorities currently deliver in building cohesive, safe and strong communities while recognizing and addressing the new challenge and threat of violent extremism. Preventing violent extremism projects are targeted projects that deal with a specific threat to support and protect vulnerable individuals within a community.

Delivering Prevent projects in ways that did not become a substitute for community cohesion was the great challenge. One that was only partially met.

In many respects, Prevent was the heir to multiculturalism: it recognizes the importance of strong community ties and strong community leadership in building resilient, empowered communities. But by doing so it places a heavy responsibility on communities that were often not yet able to exercise such control over their own, often because the very same multicultural policies have led to a significant measure of isolation (and therefore lack of development of many skills). This in turn has made them more vulnerable to both erroneous and often paranoid interpretations of world events, but perhaps more importantly even, vulnerable to remaining no more than an offshoot of politics and conflicts in the "home region" (see the relationship between politics and "home" Bangladeshi politics and nationalism in Tower Hamlets) or vulnerable to predatory ideological assaults from the likes of Saudi groups (Brixton Mosque).

Conclusion: so where are we now?

The Cameron government that came into office in 2010, immediately sought to reform the Prevent agenda, and the reformed 2011 version of Prevent has decoupled the counter-terrorism agenda from the government's "integration strategy". Prevent is firmly part of Contest, the UK's counter-terrorism strategy and located in the Home Office. Responsibility for communities and the integration agenda is shared amongst government departments, but resides mainly with a greatly reduced Department for Communities and Local Government. While this may appease some critics, it is also a rejection of many of the community-building initiatives of the previous administration. This change has resulted in the resources that had been made available for Prevent activities as community activities being reduced and more strictly allocated. *In fine*, the results are nuanced: the decoupling of the strategies has been effective in restoring a sense that community activities were not being supported merely as a way of "keeping tabs" on various community organisations. However, this has also resulted in less investment in what – counter-terrorism aside – accounts for the kind of social capital that is the bedrock of trusting community relations and cohesion.

As outlined at the beginning of this piece, we would argue that the relationship has improved and normalised: communities may have been angered and alienated, but their outspokenness and confidence in the public realm, as well as the voiced tensions within communities with respect of public policy suggests they are now more confident about making their opinions known and doing so effectively. The complexity of the situation, the multitude of dissenting voices also point to new emerging leadership, to varied media outlets, to more articulate and decisive demands. In other words, the Muslim communities are both more engaged and more confident. Conversations that never could have happened, and indeed never did are now taking place because the lines for a more authentic – because more symmetric and balanced – dialogue, however painful, have been opened.

References

Bright, M. *When Progressives Treat with Reactionaries. The British State's Flirtation with Radical Islamism.* London: Policy Exchange, 2006.

Cantle, T. *Community Cohesion: A New Framework for Race and Diversity.* London: Palgrave Macmillan, 2008.

Cantle, T. *Community Cohesion: a Report of the Independent Review Team.* London: Home Office. http://resources.cohesioninstitute.org.uk/Publications/Documents/Document/ DownloadDocumentsFile.aspx?recordId=96&file=PDFversion, 2001.

Crisp, R. and M. Hewstone. *Multiple Social Categorization: Processes, Models and Applications.* Abingdon: Psychology Press, 2006.

Parekh, B. *Rethinking Multiculturalism: Cultural Diversity and Political Theory.* London: Palgrave, 2000.

Phillips, T. "After 7/7 Sleep Walking to Segregation". Speech to the Manchester Council for Community Relations, 22 September 2005. http://www.humanities.manchester.ac.uk/social-change/research/social-change/summer-workshops/documents/sleepwalking.pdf.

Wetherell, M., M. Lafleche and R. Berkeley, eds. *Identity, Ethnic Diversity and Community Cohesion.* London: Sage, 2007.

Identity, Solidarity, and Islam in Europe

Erik Jones

Populists argue that Islamic immigrants are fundamentally different from Europeans. As evidence, they point to notions of religious and cultural identity. Such arguments have popular resonance. As more mainstream politicians pick up on these themes, they begin to take on an air of common sense. Nevertheless, they are mistaken. Europe has a long track record of reconciling competing identities. This has happened by focusing on patterns of interaction (solidarity) rather than obvious indicators of distinctiveness. Using the examples of the Netherlands and Turkey, this article illustrates the wide spectrum of European approaches to the challenge of getting different groups to share the same geographic space.

Too much of the debate about Islam and Europe focuses on questions of identity. According to the conventional wisdom, Islamic or Muslim immigrants in Europe are different from Europeans. Muslim countries are different too. Moreover, these distinctions are fundamental. The Islamic world is the 'other' to Europe's 'us'; Europeans are not like 'them'. It is no wonder, therefore, that Europeans are reluctant to see an expansion of the European Union (EU) to include Turkey or that Europeans might view Muslim immigrants as an existential threat.

This conventional wisdom is widespread.[1] It is also unconvincing. Europe's history is rich with examples of different groups that learned to live together despite their different identities. Indeed, modern Europe was founded at the end of the Thirty Years War on such a compromise. The Westphalian Peace hinged on provisions for the tolerance of religious minorities within countries with an established faith.[2] These provisions created a complex, multilayered system for regulating how

---

[1] See, for example, Caldwell, *Reflections on the Revolution in Europe.*
[2] Krasner, "Westphalia and All That"; Christin, *La paix de religion.*

different groups with different identities could interact peacefully within a shared geographic space.[3]

Examples of toleration amidst diversity are not limited to religion and can be found as easily between countries as within them. The Franco-German rapprochement at the heart of European integration is a good example. Nevertheless, Europe has a history of failure as well as success. Consider the fate of Czechoslovakia, Yugoslavia, or (possibly) Belgium.

These examples of failure are important because they suggest the difficulty in achieving and sustaining a balance between groups. Too much emphasis on uniformity is illegitimate, as Joseph Rothschild argued in his classic analysis of Central and Eastern Europe under communism, *Return to Diversity*,[4] but too much emphasis on diversity or difference is unsustainable as well, which is what Alan Milward suggested in his analysis of *The Reconstruction of Western Europe* at the end of the Second World War and *The European Rescue of the Nation-State* that came after that.[5]

Once the emphasis is on finding a balance between groups, the distinctiveness of identities loses significance.[6] Of course different groups are different. The question is how they manage to work together. This is the point made in Alberto Alesina and Enrico Spolaore's analysis of the *Size of Nations*.[7] Every country must reconcile itself to the competition between the centripetal logic of efficiency and a centrifugal logic of homogeneity. Markets depend upon a division of labour; politics upon an imagined community.[8] As a result, identity is always and necessarily compromised in the interests of solidarity.

The argument put forward in this article has four sections. The first distinguishes between identity and solidarity. The second makes the link from solidarity to organisation, using contrasting solutions to the problem of managing difference. The third introduces constraints on different formulas for reconciliation. The fourth concludes with the challenge of building confidence between groups. That challenge is common to all societies rather than unique to the relationship between Europe and the Islamic world.

Identity and solidarity

The search for group identity is synonymous with the search for community. The basic goal is to isolate those norms, values, beliefs, attitudes or affects that bind different groups of people together in a single entity. This is an important project.

---

[3] Wilson, *Europe's Tragedy.*
[4] Rothschild and Wingfield, *Return to Diversity.*
[5] Milward, *Reconstruction of Western Europe* and *European Rescue of the Nation-State.*
[6] Silvestri, "Does Islam Challenge European Identity?" and "Public Policies towards Muslims".
[7] Alesina and Spaolore, *The Size of Nations.*
[8] Anderson, *Imagined Communities.*

Nevertheless, the search for community often blurs the distinction between identity as a category of practice and identity as a category of analysis.[9] A category of practice can be used in everyday speech without confusion. The requirements for a category of analysis are much more stringent because the level of precision required is greater.

Consider the situation in Europe, where identity and community are often assumed to overlap. In practice, it makes sense to point to the existence of Europeans who both identify themselves and are identified with Europe as a collective. In analytical terms, it is more difficult to isolate what this European identity means. Self-proclaimed 'Europeans' do not all recognise each others' claim to being legitimate members of the community, they disagree over what core European values are, and they imagine different and competing visions of European unity. Hence, while Europeans exist and politicians can appeal to their European identity, that tells us very little about what Europe as a community is all about. If anything, the study of European identity reveals Europe to be a multi-layered and multifaceted construct.[10]

A similar point applies to Islamic identity and Islam. The core of the Islamic faith is perhaps more robust in terms of norms and values than the core of European identity, and yet it is also clear that considerable scope for diversity of religious devotion remains.[11] Muslims exist and can be addressed directly both as individuals and as a group. Nevertheless, Muslim identity as a category for analysis is rich in potential for ambiguity and error.[12]

The challenge is to find some alternative analytical framework. This is the problem that Rogers Brubaker and Frederick Cooper place at the centre of their attempt to move "beyond 'identity'".[13] Given the many meanings of identity as a concept, Brubaker and Cooper call for a new analytic placeholder that includes three elements: "categorical commonality", "relational connectedness", and "a feeling of belonging together". This is only a subset of identity-related concerns. Nevertheless, it is less prone to ambiguity than the broader notion of identity and it is more narrowly focused on community building. The goal is:

> to develop an analytical idiom sensitive to the multiple forms and degrees of commonality and connectedness, and to the widely varying ways in which actors (and the cultural idioms, public narratives, and prevailing discourses on which they draw) attribute meaning and significance to them. This will enable us to distinguish instances of strongly binding, vehemently felt groupness from more loosely structured, weakly constraining forms of affinity and affiliation.[14]

---

[9] Brubaker and Cooper, "Beyond 'Identity'", 4–6.
[10] Risse, *A Community of Europeans?*
[11] Hassan, *Inside Muslim Minds*; Ramadan, *Radical Reform.*
[12] Cox and Marks, *The West, Islam and Islamism*; Silvestri, "Public Policies towards Muslims".
[13] Brubaker and Cooper, "Beyond 'Identity'".
[14] *Ibid.*, 20–1.

Brubaker and Cooper choose not to give a single name to this idiom. "Solidarity" is sufficient to achieve their analytical objectives.

Identity and solidarity are closely connected as concepts. Nevertheless, while identity is a broad, encompassing concept reflecting both the nature of the individual and the constitution of groups, solidarity is more precisely focused on how individuals or groups interact. The shorter edition of the *Oxford English Dictionary* (*OED*) gives three definitions for solidarity. The first is an expression of a sense of belonging: "Unity or accordance of feeling, action, etc., esp. among individuals with common interest, sympathies, or aspirations ... ; mutual support or cohesiveness within a group". The second is categorical: "Complete or exact coincidence of interests". The third is relational: "A form of obligation involving joint and several responsibilities or rights". The ordering is not the same as that posited by Brubaker and Cooper, but the content is equivalent.

As an analytical category, solidarity is less encompassing than identity. It also offers the capacity to distinguish between different types of groups and inter-group relationships that Brubaker and Cooper seek. Solidarity gives both a measure of intensity and a range of alternative expressions. One way to consider this would be to imagine a spectrum like that suggested by Karl Deutsch and his colleagues in their study of the formation of security communities.[15] At one end of the spectrum, groups with little interaction have little common understanding or shared experience. At the other end, intensive interaction leads to greater recognition and deeper bonds of affinity. Moreover, as groups progress from one extreme to another through a growing intensity of their interaction, they acquire the ability to build bridging institutions and make binding commitments. In its extreme form, this is how language groups, ethnic groups and nations are created.[16] And if solidarity is absent at one end of the spectrum, it reaches its extreme at the other.

In the context of community-building or nation-building, this notion of solidarity is flexible enough to use in analysing multiple forms of organisation. Consider four examples. An alliance made in the face of an existential threat can work on the basis that 'the enemy of my enemy is my friend', which is an apt description of the solidarity that existed between the United Kingdom and the Soviet Union during the Second World War. The same is not true of a market relationship where the emphasis is more squarely centred on rights and obligations: as Gunnar Myrdal argued, solidarity exists in the market when everyone agrees to abide by the same rules.[17] Identity would not be of much use in either context; solidarity would.

Distributive arrangements offer a third illustration of solidarity in practice. The welfare state emerged out of the recognition by different groups in society that they

---

[15] Deutsch *et al.*, *Political Community and the North Atlantic Area*.
[16] See also Luttwak, *Grand Strategy of the Byzantine Empire*.
[17] Myrdal, *An International Economy*, 22.

faced different challenges: social unrest for some, poverty and insecurity for others. At the same time, the architects of the welfare state realised that any common solution would generate different outcomes for different classes: some would contribute, others would benefit. The formulas for welfare state development differ considerably from one country to the next and yet all such formulas express solidarity both in terms of inter-group affinity and in terms of rights and obligations.[18]

A common foreign policy offers a fourth expression of solidarity. It is one thing for different groups to bind together in response to a common existential threat, it is quite another for groups to send their members abroad to die for some less existential purpose. The NATO alliance wrestled with this distinction in the 'out of area' debate and during operations in Afghanistan.

Of course solidarity is not the only possible analytic construct for tackling the problems raised by Brubaker and Cooper.[19] The literature is rich with alternatives. Thomas Risse focuses on the processes that lie beneath the social construction of identities; Neil Fligstein looks at indicators for interaction and language use; Peter Kraus examines patterns of linguistic diversity; Jeffrey Checkel and Peter Katzenstein pull together contributors from different disciplines to benefit from their methodological and epistemological plurality.[20] Each of these approaches promises to strengthen the use of identity as an analytic category. Each does so, however, by narrowing its conceptual ambit to focus on a specific problematic.[21]

The concept of solidarity is similarly focused. The goal in using this concept is to understand how different groups can share the same public institutions and geographic resources. This is not exclusively a challenge for nation-building. In many cases, as in Europe today, the polities already exist and the communities are struggling to deal with new entrants or cleavages. The challenge is to work out how these differences can be reconciled.

Accommodation and assimilation

One way to illustrate the range of possible formulas for the reconciliation of groups with different identities but sharing the same geographic space is to look at the extremes, with the accommodation of difference at one end of the spectrum and assimilation at the other end. There are a number of possible examples of each strategy. The Netherlands and Turkey offer one possible illustration of 'most different' cases. What they have in common is the need to reconcile competing

---

[18] See, for example, Anderson, *Imagined Communities*.
[19] Brubaker and Cooper, "Beyond 'Identity'".
[20] Risse, *A Community of Europeans?*; Fligstein, *Euro-Clash*; Kraus, *A Union of Diversity*; Checkel and Katzenstein, *European Identity*.
[21] Jones, "Identity and Solidarity".

religious groups (or, as Hans Daalder referred to them, political subcultures[22]). They differ in almost every other respect. The Netherlands is an example of accommodation; Turkey exemplifies assimilation. These national formulas for reconciliation arguably worked best during a period that runs from the 1920s and 1930s until sometime in the 1960s or 1970s. They are no longer so effective. Why those strategies broke down is the subject of the next section. For now, the goal is to survey how they functioned.

The Dutch model is called consociational democracy.[23] Within that model, different religious groups in Dutch society – Catholic, Protestant, and non-confessional – accepted to live separate lives while sharing the same geographic space. This acceptance was facilitated by the existence (or development) of parallel and redundant social institutions. Each group had its own schools, hospitals, universities, media and the like. Acceptance of diversity was also enforced by elites using hierarchical institutions such as trade unions, employers associations and political parties to guide a largely deferent public. Finally, the whole system was undergirded by processes of elite socialisation as individuals moved up through the ranks of hierarchical structures and by clear social norms against fraternisation across groups. This made it possible for elites to negotiate with one another and then enforce the terms of any bargain from the top down. The only requirement was that everyone should abide by the rules of the game.[24]

The Dutch experience with consociational democracy was often difficult. Some groups, such as the communists (atheists), refused to accept the terms of accommodation; others, such as the more fundamentalist Protestants, opted to isolate themselves from the rest. By and large, however, the Dutch pattern for accommodation generated sufficient stability and prosperity to force scholars to reconsider fundamentally whether the mere existence of strong differences between groups is inherently unstable. Hence, even after the model broke down in the Netherlands, its application elsewhere remained of interest.[25]

The Turkish approach to reconciling religious differences stressed assimilation rather than accommodation. Soon after taking power, Mustafa Kemal, more commonly known as Atatürk, created a distinction between religion and public life. He also fostered an encompassing, pro-Western, Turkish national identity. The adjustments he demanded were much harder for some groups than others. He banned Alevi worship and Sufi devotional practices, prohibited traditional dress (like the fez) and the use of Kurdish languages, restricted the outward display of (Sunni)

---

[22] Daalder, "The Consociational Democracy Theme".
[23] Lijphart, *The Politics of Accommodation* and "Consociational Democracy".
[24] Daalder, "The Consociational Democracy Theme".
[25] Steiner and Ertman, "Consociationalism and Corporatism in Western Europe".

Islamic devotion, introduced a Latin script, and insisted on having the call to prayer in Turkish rather than Arabic.[26]

Non-Islamic groups in Turkey received different treatment as well. The crimes committed against Armenian Christians during the waning years of the Ottoman empire were not acknowledged. As a result, Armenian Christians were unable to claim restitution and they continued to suffer from discrimination and persecution.[27] According to the 1923 Lausanne Treaty, however, Armenian, Orthodox and Syriac Christians were recognised as religious minorities, as were members of the Jewish faith. This recognition did not eliminate state discrimination against non-Islamic minorities, particularly through the selective taxation or capital levies. It also carried an implicit injunction against conversion.[28] Nevertheless, official recognition of religious minorities implied acceptance that they would remain in Turkey alongside the Turks. Despite the strong secular line of the new government, the association between Islam and Turkishness, non-Muslim and minority remained.[29]

The contrast between the Netherlands and Turkey is striking. In the Dutch formula, different religious groups had to remain distinctive for the system to function; they also had to interact in broadly prescribed patterns of behaviour. As a result, the elites involved in bargaining across groups began to identify with the system as a whole.[30] Hence, it was not uncommon in the Netherlands to talk about consociational political parties or – in a closely related sense – corporatist elites. On the contrary, these words, together with the term used to describe the vertically organised social and political system, *verzuiling* or 'pillarisation', were part of the conventional speech you might see reported in the newspaper. In the Turkish formula, by contrast, differences between groups were minimized if not obliterated. For much of the history of the Turkish Republic, official speech denied the very existence of Alevi or, more importantly, Kurdish minorities; it openly embraced the constraints of secularism on the country's Islamic heritage; and it rewrote the history of the Turkish people as a nation.[31]

Despite these differences, both the Dutch and the Turkish formulas relied heavily on top-down enforcement mechanisms. Moreover, in the Netherlands as in Turkey, the goal was stability and not repression. Both the Dutch and the Turkish formulas for solidarity were forged in moments of existential threat, where domestic division in the face of external challenges risked bringing an abrupt end to the country. Using the *OED* definition of solidarity, the practice

---

[26] Lewis, *The Emergence of Modern Turkey*, 403–10, 425–30; Robinson, *The First Turkish Republic*, 79–87.
[27] De Bellaigue, *Rebel Land*; Bobellian, *Children of Armenia*.
[28] Even today the Church of Jesus Christ of Latter Day Saints has gained limited recognition from the Turkish state with the tacit agreement that it would not openly seek converts.
[29] Lewis, *The Emergence of Modern Turkey*, 350; Bein, *Ottoman Ulema*.
[30] Koole and Daalder, "The Consociational Democracy Model".
[31] Öktem, *Angry Nation*, 14–55; Özbudun, "Turkey – Plural Society and Monolithic State".

of accommodation or assimilation was intended to create unity and cohesion, to realign and harmonise disparate interests, to create rights and to enforce obligations. Only in this way would it be possible to persevere in the face of adversity. As Bernard Lewis explained with respect to Turkey: "The best hope for the future lay in the sometimes painful emergence, out of all the groups, of the individual – better informed and more self-reliant, with a growing awareness of his place, his rights, and his duties in a free modern society."[32]

The motivation to pursue such extreme measures for social unity in the Netherlands and in Turkey continued long after the dissipation of any existential threat. In turn, social unity became a bulwark for longer-term projects of modernisation and industrialisation. Despite their differences, both countries experienced profound economic and social adjustments during the middle of the 20th century. Along the way, Dutch and Turkish elites used different formulas for solidarity – accommodation in the Netherlands and assimilation in Turkey – to harness the power of groups and individuals to the common cause of development.

The Dutch story began with efforts to ensure an "equitable distribution of poverty" after the ravages of the Second World War and succeeded by the early 1960s in achieving a rapid rise in income per capita and the virtual elimination of unemployment.[33] The Turkish economy's development over the same period was similarly dramatic in relative if not absolute terms. Turkey could not claim to have raised per capita incomes to the levels of Western Europe nor could it yet even aspire to the elimination of the widespread underemployment that plagued much of Anatolia. Nevertheless, Turkey could make a credible application for eventual membership in the European Economic Community, culminating in the negotiation of the 1963 Ankara Agreement, an agreement which recognises the fact "that the support given by the European Economic Community to the efforts of the Turkish people to improve their standard of living will facilitate the accession of Turkey to the Community at a later date". The practical effects of the Ankara Agreement were limited, at least in the short- to medium-term, but its importance as a symbol of Turkish achievement should not be underestimated.[34]

Solidarity, discipline, confidence and prejudice

Neither accommodation nor assimilation proved sustainable over time. The signs of weakness in both models for solidarity were evident almost from the outset. The problem is that both accommodation and assimilation require high levels of discipline, as individuals accept instruction from their elites. They require high levels of confidence among both individuals and elites in the capacity of the system to

[32] Lewis, *The Emergence of Modern Turkey*, 355.
[33] Van Zanden, *Economic History of the Netherlands*.
[34] Müftüler-Baç and Stivachtis, *Turkey-European Union Relations*.

regulate other groups. And they must overcome the prejudice that other groups will seek to shunt aside the burdens of necessary adjustment or manipulate the system to accrue a disproportionate share of any gains. When groups lack discipline, they cannot fulfil their obligations; when they lack confidence, they feel a sense of disadvantage or injustice more strongly than a sense of belonging; and when they experience prejudice, they exaggerate points of difference and look for ways to use whatever resources are available to bend the system in defence of their own interests. Such constraints are inherent to the notion of solidarity as the *OED* defines it, and they proved binding in both the Netherlands and Turkey.

A major problem in the Netherlands was the loss of discipline through the decline in religious devotion and the weakening of party allegiance.[35] Voters did not switch their preference from Catholic to Protestant, but – as the role of religion diminished in Dutch society over time – voters did switch from confessional to liberal or social democrat (meaning Labour Party). They also began to mobilise against the consociational system altogether, forging new political identities as 'democrats' in the pluralist sense of the term. And they began to move across boundaries in other aspects of the vertical social pillars, changing employer alliances or trade union memberships, attending different universities, and experimenting with different kinds of personal relationships. This forced elites to compete for support rather than take their followers for granted. In turn, competition between elites made it harder for them to engage in inter-group bargaining where consensus and compromise are the predominant norms. It also gave rise to new cross-group institutional forms like a common trade union federation or a combined Catholic and Protestant political party, the Christian Democratic Appeal (CDA).[36]

The situation in Turkey was reversed. For many of the larger minorities, the willingness to accept the discipline of the state quickly wore thin. The Kurds wanted to break free from the common Turkish ethnicity, Alevi and Sufi groups wanted to regain their right to worship, and more conservative elements in the Sunni majority sought to bring religious values back into the public sphere. In turn, this shook the confidence of the secular elites (and specifically the military) in the resilience of the democratic system and strengthened their prejudice that the country would be thrown backward both economically and politically should the Islamists or the separatists be unleashed.[37] From the standpoint of the minority groups involved, the prior judgment (or biased attitudes) of Turkish secular elites was harmful and injurious in the sense that minorities believed their rights were disregarded; from the standpoint of the military itself, the prejudice was nothing more than an anticipatory judgment, "a preconceived idea of what will happen",

---

[35] Koole and Daalder, "The Consociational Democracy Model".
[36] Andeweg and Irwin, *Governance and Politics of the Netherlands*, 43–68.
[37] Öktem, *Angry Nation*, 84–121.

and they were unwilling to experiment in order to test its validity. These two different dimensions of prejudice sit uneasily side by side. As a result, the country experienced a long cycle of civil unrest punctuated with episodes of military dictatorship.[38]

The irony in both the Dutch and Turkish cases is that the success of economic and political development nurtured the rejection of the accommodation or assimilation that was used to undergird modernisation in the first place. The point here is not that people in either country would have been content to live in such constraining systems had economic development not taken place. It is worth reiterating that problems with both systems started almost from the beginning. In this sense, rising relative prosperity was not a necessary precondition for rebellion against the constraints of either system. Prosperity just made reform easier to initiate and more difficult to resist.[39]

The Dutch story centres on the anti-consociational movements, the most successful of which was the Democrats '66 (D66) political party. D66 developed as part of the wider value change and electoral transformation that took place across Western Europe in the 1960s and 1970s.[40] It drew support from a young, highly educated, middle-class electorate, which waxed and waned in its attention to national politics (and allegiance to the party) through the end of the twentieth century. When it was strongest in the early 1990s, D66 helped to oust the CDA from its hegemonic position at the centre of Dutch politics. Once in power, however, D66 became associated with the practice of elite consensus and so ceded ground to movements and political parties that promised a more radical break with the past. The dramatic success of charismatic populists like Pim Fortuyn, who led his eponymous list to prominence in the 2002 elections, and to a lesser extent Jan Marijnissen, who led the Socialist Party to make significant gains in 2006, was the result. By the early twenty-first century, Dutch politicians from across the political spectrum openly rejected the central tenets of consociational democracy:[41] they embraced a common national identity rather than remaining wedded to narrower sub-national political cultures and they focused much more attention on assimilation than accommodation. Indeed, in the extreme form, right-wing xenophobes like Geert Wilders and Rita Verdonk talk of little else.[42] The view of social solidarity they offer is very different from the accommodation practiced in the past. Immigrants must become more 'Dutch' if they are to be accepted as part of Dutch society; they cannot expect to share the crowded

---

[38] See, for example, *ibid.* and Jenkins, *Political Islam in Turkey*.

[39] Jones, *Economic Adjustment and Political Transformation*; Atasoy, *Islam's Marriage with Neoliberalism*.

[40] Inglehart, *Silent Revolution*.

[41] Keman, "Politics in the Netherlands after 1989".

[42] Blok and van Melle, *Veel gekker kan het niet worden*. For more detail, see the article by van Genugten in this issue, 72.

geographic space of the Netherlands if they insist on stressing their differences from the rest of the country.

The Turkish story centres on the rise of political Islam. Although violent clashes with Kurdish separatists may have captured the lion's share of popular and press attention in the 1980s and 1990s, it was the emergence and consolidation of an increasingly prosperous and conservative Anatolian middle class that brought about the most significant transformation of the Turkish state.[43] State concessions in the 1940s allowed the creation of Islamic educational institutions to provide for better trained religious officials – *imam* to lead the call to prayer, *hatip* to give the sermons, and hence Imam-Hatip schools. Meanwhile, the teachings of Fethullah Gülen gave impetus to devout Muslims to seek the benefits of education as a means of reconciling the challenges of modernisation and the requirements of the Islamic faith.[44] By the 1980s, it became possible for graduates of Imam-Hatip schools to survive the fiercely competitive national entrance exams to go to university. Together with followers of the Gülen movement, these graduates developed into a highly educated and self-confident parallel Turkish elite. This more religiously conservative elite was not always unified, particularly as regards the legitimacy of the secular state, but it was nevertheless committed to seeking greater freedom for expression of religious devotion in the public space.[45]

By 1995 an openly Islamist party was able to capture a plurality of the electorate and in 1996 this group was able to put forward one of its own members as prime minister. The reaction of the military was precipitous. When the pro-Islamist prime minister began making changes that could challenge the secular basis of the Turkish state, he was ousted, his party was banned, and new rules were passed to close off the route to university via Imam-Hatip schools in order to slow down the growth of the parallel, religiously conservative elite. Such efforts proved to be too little, too late. The conservative and yet not explicitly Islamist Justice and Development Party (AKP) that emerged from the experience of the 1990s was able to win a controlling majority in parliament in 2002. It took time for this party to consolidate its position and there were tense encounters with the military and the judiciary along the way. Nevertheless it was able to challenge fundamentally the secular basis of the Turkish state, to reconsider the treatment of both Alevi and Kurdish minorities, and to shift attention from assimilation to accommodation.[46] The notion of solidarity promoted by the AKP is very different because it does not depend upon adherence to the strong and encompassing idea of Turkish identity espoused by Atatürk. Both ethnic and religious minorities can be

---

[43] Yavuz, *Islamic Political Identity in Turkey* and *Secularism and Muslim Democracy*.
[44] Koyuncu Lorasdaği, "Globalization, Modernization, and Democratization".
[45] Fuller, *The New Turkish Republic*, 56–66; Atasoy *Islam's Marriage with Neoliberalism*.
[46] Öktem, *Angry Nation*.

different from the Sunni Turkish mainstream and yet still participate in Turkish society and remain loyal to the Turkish state.

These thumbnail sketches show how both extreme forms for managing religious differences had to yield to moderation. The accommodating Dutch became more intent on assimilation,[47] the assimilating Turks learned to accept the inevitability of some form of accommodation.[48] The adjustment is difficult in both cases. The Dutch struggle to master their own xenophobic tendencies as well as the disillusionment and disaffection of Muslim minority groups; the Turks wrestle with the prospect that pro-Islamist reforms might get carried away.

Conclusion: relationships first

The differences between European and Islamic identities will always exist. Even with extensive powers of coercion, it would be impossible to change that fact. That is what the history of modern Turkey has to teach us. Attempting to accommodate those differences by creating separate parallel and redundant social structures will not resolve the tension either. Under the best of circumstances, that is the lesson from the Netherlands. Under more austere conditions, we need only look at South Africa. *Verzuiling* was no more stable as a long-term prospect than *apartheid*. That leaves little alternative but to keep looking for ways to reconcile differences so that different groups can live peacefully together.

The problem of integrating Islam into Europe cannot be resolved by focusing on identity politics. This holds whether the subject is immigration into Europe or the accession of Turkey to the European Union.[49] Identity is important in understanding such challenges, but the solution must be found by focusing on relations between groups rather than on their cultural distinctiveness.

Part of the explanation lies in the ambiguity of identity as an analytic construct. That is the argument made by Brubaker and Cooper.[50] However, a larger part of the explanation lies in the difficulty of translating cultural values into social and political institutions. The Turkish experiment with assimilation failed because minority groups in Turkey never accepted the state as legitimate and because confessional politicians chafed at the constraints implied by the secular state. The Dutch experiment with accommodation failed because both religious devotion and elite deference proved to be wasting assets.

Focusing attention on solidarity rather than identity offers two distinct advantages. To begin with, it is possible not to prioritise common interests over distinctive characteristics. It is also possible to tailor relationships to specific contexts.

---

[47] Joppke, "Beyond National Models", 5–9.
[48] Cizre, "A New Politics of Engagement".
[49] Bogdani, *Turkey and EU Accession.*
[50] Brubaker and Cooper, "Beyond 'Identity'".

Turkish Islamists can embrace religious pluralism as well as free markets; Dutch Protestants and Catholics can support either right or left. The point here is not to suggest that all combinations are possible and that voters are free to float between them. Rather it is to argue that even very high levels of electoral volatility might be bounded by competing conceptions of appropriateness.[51]

References

Alesina, A. and E. Spolaore. *The Size of Nations*. Cambridge: MIT Press, 2005.

Anderson, B. *Imagined Communities: Reflections on the Origin and Spread of Nationalism*, Revised Edition. London: Verso, 1991.

Andeweg, R.B. and G.A. Irwin. *Governance and Politics of the Netherlands*. Basingstoke: Palgrave, 2002.

Atasoy, Y. *Islam's Marriage with Neoliberalism: State Transformation in Turkey*. Basingstoke: Palgrave, 2009.

Bein, A. *Ottoman Ulema, Turkish Republic: Agents of Change and Guardians of Tradition*. Stanford: Stanford University Press, 2011.

Blok, A. and J. van Melle. *Veekl gekker kan het niet worden*. Hilversum: Just Publishers, 2008.

Bobelian, M. *Children of Armenia: A Forgotten Genocide and the Century-Long Struggle for Justice*. New York: Simon & Schuster, 2009.

Bogdani, M. *Turkey and the Dilemma of EU Accession: When Religion Meets Politics*. London: I.B. Taurus, 2011.

Brubaker, R. and F. Cooper. "Beyond 'Identity'". *Theory and Society* 29, no. 1 (February 2000): 1–47.

Caldwell, C. *Reflections on the Revolution in Europe: Immigration, Islam, and the West*. New York: Doubleday, 2009.

Checkel, J.T. and P.J. Katzenstein, eds. *European Identity*. Cambridge: Cambridge University Press, 2009.

Christin, O. *La paix de religion: L'autonomisation de la raison politique au XVIe siècle*. Paris: Éditions du Seuil, 1997.

Cizre, Ü. "A New Politics of Engagement: The Turkish Military, Society, and the AKP". In *Democracy, Islam, and Secularism in Turkey*, edited by A.T. Kuru and A. Stepan: 122–48. New York: Columbia University Press, 2012.

Cox, C. and J. Marks. *The West, Islam and Islamism: Is Ideological Islam Compatible with Liberal Democracy?* 2nd ed. London: Civitas, 2006.

Daalder, H. "The Consociational Democracy Theme". *World Politics* 26, no. 4 (July 1974): 604–21.

De Bellaigue, C. *Rebel Land: Among Turkey's Forgotten People*. London: Bloomsbury, 2009.

Deutsch, K.W., S.A. Burrell, R.A. Kann and M. Lee. *Political Community and the North Atlantic Area: International Organization in the Light of Historical Experience*. Princeton: Princeton University Press, 1957.

Fligstein, N. *Euro-Clash: The EU, European Identity, and the Future of Europe*. Oxford: Oxford University Press, 2008.

Fuller, G.E. *The New Turkish Republic: Turkey as a Pivotal State in the Muslim World*. Washington, DC: United States Institute of Peace, 2008.

Hassan, R. *Inside Muslim Minds*. Melbourne: Melbourne University Press, 2008.

---

[51] Van der Meer *et al.* "Bounded Volatility".

Inglehart, R. *Silent Revolution: Changing Values and Political Styles among Western Publics*. Princeton: Princeton University Press, 1977.

Jenkins, G. *Political Islam in Turkey: Running West, Heading East*. London: Palgrave, 2008.

Jones, E. "Identity and Solidarity". In *The Oxford Handbook of the European Union*, edited by E. Jones, A. Menon and S. Weatherill: 690–702. Oxford: Oxford University Press, 2012.

Jones, E. *Economic Adjustment and Political Transformation in Small States*. Oxford: Oxford University Press, 2008.

Joppke, C. "Beyond National Models: Civic Integration Policies for Immigrants in Western Europe". *West European Politics* 30, no. 1 (January 2007): 1–22.

Keman, H. "Introduction: Politics in the Netherlands after 1989: A Final Farewell to Consociationalism?" *Acta Politica* 43, no. 2–3 (July 2008): 149–53.

Koole, R. and H. Daalder. "The Consociational Democracy Model and the Netherlands: Ambivalent Allies?" *Acta Politica* 37, special issue (Spring/Summer 2002): 23–43.

Koyuncu Lorasdaği, B. "Globalization, Modernization, and Democratization in Turkey: The Fetullah Güllen Movement". In *Remaking Turkey: Globalization, Alternative Modernities, and Democracy*, edited by E.F. Keyman: 153–77. Lanham: Lexington Books, 2007.

Krasner, S.D. "Westphalia and All That". In *Ideas and Foreign Policy: Beliefs, Institutions, and Political Change*, edited by J. Goldstein and R.O. Keohane: 235–64. Ithaca, NY: Cornell University Press, 1993.

Kraus, P.A. *A Union of Diversity: Language, Identity, and Polity-building in Europe*. Cambridge: Cambridge University Press, 2008.

Lewis, B. *The Emergence of Modern Turkey*. Oxford: Oxford University Press, 1961.

Lijphart, A. *The Politics of Accommodation: Pluralism and Democracy in the Netherlands*. 2nd ed. Berkeley: University of California Press, 1982.

Lijphart, A. "Consociational Democracy". *World Politics* 21, no. 2 (January 1969): 207–25.

Luttwak, E. *The Grand Strategy of the Byzantine Empire*. Cambridge: Harvard University Press, 2009.

Milward, A.S. *The European Rescue of the Nation-State*. London: Routledge, 1992.

Milward, A. *The Reconstruction of Western Europe: 1945–51*. London: Routledge, 1984.

Müftüler-Baç, M. and Y.A. Stivachtis, eds. *Turkey-European Union Relations: Dilemmas, Opportunities: Constraints*. Lanham: Lexington Books, 2008.

Myrdal, G. *An International Economy: Problems: Prospects*. New York: Harper & Brothers, 1956.

Öktem, K. *Angry Nation: Turkey Since 1989*. London: Zed Books, 2011.

Özbudun, E. "Turkey – Plural Society and Monolithic State". In *Democracy, Islam and Secularism in Turkey*, edited by A.T. Kuru and A. Stepan: 61–94. New York: Columbia University Press, 2012.

Ramadan, T. *Radical Reform: Islamic Ethics and Liberation*. Oxford: Oxford University Press, 2008.

Risse, T. *A Community of Europeans? Transnational Identities and Public Spheres*. Ithaca, NY: Cornell University Press, 2010.

Robinson, R.D. *The First Turkish Republic: A Case Study in National Development*. Cambridge: Harvard University Press, 1963.

Rothschild, J. and N.M. Wingfield. *Return to Diversity: A Political History of East Central Europe Since World War II*. 3rd ed. Oxford: Oxford University Press, 2000.

Silvestri, S. "Public Policies towards Muslims and the Institutionalization of 'Moderate Islam' in Europe". In *Muslims in 21st Century Europe*, edited by A. Triandafyllidou: 45–58. London: Routledge, 2010.

Silvestri, S. "Does Islam Challenge European Identity?" In *The Religious Roots of Contemporary European Identity*, edited by L. Faltin and M.J. Wright: 14–28. London: Continuum, 2007.

Steiner, J, and T. Ertman, eds. "Consociationalism and Corporatism in Western Europe: Still the Politics of Accommodation?" *Acta Politica* 37, special issue (Spring/Summer 2002).

Van der Meer, T., R. Lubbe, E. van Elsas, M. Elff and W. van der Brug. "Bounded Volatility in the Dutch Electoral Battlefield: A Panel Study on the Structure of Changing Vote Intentions in the Netherlands during 2006–2010". *Acta Politica* 47, no. 4 (October 2012): 333–55.

Van Zanden, J.L. *The Economic History of the Netherlands, 1914–1995: A Small Open Economy in the "Long" Twentieth Century.* London: Routledge, 1998.

Wilson, P.H. *Europe's Tragedy: A History of the Thirty Years War.* London: Allen Lane, 2009.

Yavuz, M.H. *Secularism and Muslim Democracy in Turkey.* Cambridge: Cambridge University Press, 2009.

Yavuz, M.H. *Islamic Political Identity in Turkey.* Oxford: Oxford University Press, 2003.

Index

Note: Page numbers followed by "n" denote notes.

INDEX

www.ingramcontent.com/pod-product-compliance
Ingram Content Group UK Ltd.
Pitfield, Milton Keynes, MK11 3LW, UK
UKHW010021280225
455677UK00023B/725